"Gripping stories, unpretentious wisdom, and down-to-earth God-talk: This is an indispensable guidebook for activists who need reactivating. When your hope flags, grab this book and read!"
— Catherine Keller, Drew Theological School, author of *Political Theology of the Earth [Our Planetary Emergency and the Struggle for a New Public]*

"Murphy has thought deeply and honestly as he lived out his calling to liberate and seek justice. Other Christian activists will resonate to much that he has said. He recognizes unflinchingly the depth of resistance to reform from others, from the system, and from our own weariness and despair. In the context of repeated failure and hopeless odds, he calls us to keep on keeping on. We are not likely to be victorious. But our faithfulness will make a difference, a difference worth making. Thank you, Tim, for calling us, without self-deception or false expectation of divine intervention, to lives of faithfulness, hopefulness, and love."
— John B. Cobb Jr., founding codirector of Center for Process Studies and Process & Faith

"Tim Murphy's new book is just what I needed. If you need encouragement, perspective, and solid reasons to keep going in the struggle for justice, get *Sustaining Hope in an Unjust World.*"
— Brian McLaren, author and activist

SUSTAINING HOPE IN AN UNJUST WORLD

HOW TO KEEP GOING WHEN YOU WANT TO GIVE UP

Timothy Charles Murphy

chalice
press

Saint Louis, Missouri

An imprint of Christian Board of Publication

Cover design: Ponderosa Pine Design.
Cover art: Adaptation of "Girl silhouette holding a giant ball" by Chuwy, ©shutterstock.com.

ChalicePress.com

Print: 9780827235434

EPUB: 9780827235441

EPDF: 9780827235458

Printed in the United States of America

*To all co-travelers who struggle mightily for
a more just and peaceful world.*

Contents

Prologue

It was a cancer diagnosis that made me to come to grips with the fact that things do not always turn out all right. In spite of such potential failure, I also learned how we can keep the faith in the midst of seemingly insurmountable struggles for a better world.

I was 19, depressed, with no appetite, and in constant pain. For the previous six months, my health had been declining slowly. First, it was the chronic back pain. The doctors said I had pulled a muscle, so I did stretches, took pain pills, and waited in vain for some improvement. Then, I became nauseous when eating. Instead of my previous voluminous appetite, I felt stuffed after half a sandwich. Months went by. The perpetual pain wore on my psyche.

Finally, after talking repeatedly with doctors who brushed my situation aside, a new doctor and I finally agreed: I had testicular cancer. Knowing what was wrong helped a lot. So did the surgery and later chemotherapy. But before that, something else happened: my pastor came over to my family's house. He asked me how I felt, whether I was struggling with God's role, and wondered what was on my mind and heart. With his encouragement, I told him I knew that this wasn't something that God had given me as a punishment, or a test, or for any other reason. Cancer happens. The only question was the following: what would I do in response to this situation?

During my stint with chemo treatments, I didn't dwell on the odds. But later my father told me that, statistically speaking, I had had only a 50/50 shot at surviving what was an advanced stage of cancer. While my family and I focused on getting through months of treatment, I understood that there was no guarantee that I would get better. God wasn't controlling this process, and, while some cancer patients improve, some don't. Fortunately, I did, and after the first surgery my nausea went away and I began regaining previously lost weight.

However, this isn't a book about cancer. It's about how we can understand the Divine in our world—what God does, and what God doesn't do—and how we are to respond. I tell the story because this experience fundamentally shaped and shapes my views of the world. But instead of giving me only a sense of personal meaning amidst such tragedy, this experience gradually led me to a different conclusion— that, in spite of no proof that things will get better, we can sustain hope in an unjust world. In fact, being faithful to the dream of a just world is enough, even if we don't fully achieve it. Before becoming sick, and increasingly afterward, I was regularly outraged about social inequities—people being mistreated, violence against the weak, crushing poverty, etc. I wasn't much of an activist at the time, but my trajectory was a proto-radical one (by Western Kentucky standards, at least!), partly because I had experienced significant marginalization and bullying as a child in school.

Over the years, as I have become more engaged in issues of social justice, activism, public policy, and the role of faith for social transformation, I've found that my worldview frequently clashes with the prevailing assumptions of my religious and secular activist peers. Almost everyone combines their recognition of the *need* for a victory against oppression and evil with the guarantee of that victory, at least rhetorically. But here's the rub: we often lose. Movements falter. Evil triumphs.

Don't get me wrong: I am not arguing that we are guaranteed to lose. Nor am I against the idea of winning. I'm against the assumption that we are guaranteed to win. Of course, just as there is no guarantee that we—as individuals, a society, or a planet—will win and triumph, there is no guarantee we will lose. Some things may get better, like gender equity, while wealth disparities get worse. I freely admit that this is a hard pill to swallow. Various psychological studies have shown that if there is one thing people on the whole dislike, it's uncertainty. This is not the uncertainty of, "I don't have an opinion." It's more like scientific uncertainty. If we know something terrible is going to happen and there's nothing we can do about it, we can resign ourselves to that fate and move on. But *uncertainty* creates in most people a sense of paralysis. For myself, it was better to know that I had advanced cancer, with the possibility of fatal consequences, than just to feel terrible and not know what was going on. We humans crave predictability, or at least some sense of knowledge and control.

In the midst of so much injustice, how can we continue to struggle for a better world, with all the effort that will be necessary for that possible future to have a fighting chance, if there are no guarantees? What if I told you that God doesn't guarantee our victory in the struggle for social justice? That God doesn't guarantee that we will win?

Instead of a promise that everything is going to be just as God intends, what if God's promise is *to be with us no matter what*? Could we then take these terrible problems we face and respond with steadfast compassion? Would that be enough? Could we keep up the struggle in the face of so much injustice and evil in our world? Could it be that the promise of God with us, come what may, is in fact enough? If so, we would have the beginnings of how to keep going when we want to give up.

1

For the Love of Social Activism

This is a book about faith. It is a book about social justice activism. But more than anything, this is a book about how to maintain hope even when we lose. Being engaged in social justice activism isn't about being a Democrat, Republican, or something else. It's about sharing good news, or a gospel, that frees people from oppression. Such a gospel leads us to a place filled with justice, peace, and compassion. We could call these values anti-racist, eco-centric, feminist, queer-affirming, democratic socialism, or a whole bunch of other things. Even if we use different labels or images or emphasize certain issues before others, there are millions of us who share this dream, this hope of freedom from oppression. Let's call it a progressive agenda. For the broad camp of people who would by and large get on board with this values list, this book is for you.

With so many oppressions to tackle, perhaps the first challenge is on where to focus our energies. Unlike right-wing activists, who tend to have a narrower constellation of concerns—namely restricting rights as they relate to sexuality, reducing government programs on social services, and expanding U.S. military dominance (the Trump coalition has added more explicit white identity grievances), more left-leaning communities have dozens of issues that pull groups in many different directions.

This was a tendency I saw at work at a progressive church I once served. Out of a membership of around three hundred people, approximately 30 self-identified as activists. Among that group, there were at least 20 issues that people cared about. Members focused variously on winter housing for the homeless, HIV/AIDS support, the immediate needs of undocumented workers in fields, undocumented workers doing long-term organizing, labor rights, children visiting their parents in prison, anti-war protests—and on and on. We struggled with how the church could do things collectively. Though it was a good thing that each person was empowered to work on their particular passion, the challenge was that it left us somewhat scattered. There were a million demands, all vying for attention. Some actions would be on the same day as an action for another issue, both seeking volunteers from the same pool of people. Recruiting for *this* issue could feel like it was sapping energy for another. Coordinating our disparate passions was a constant struggle. If you weren't working directly on someone's specific issue, at times it could lead to problems and hurt feelings.

I saw a similar dynamic when I was the executive director at the social justice nonprofit Progressive Christians Uniting (PCU). People run with the issue that touches their hearts. For a nonprofit that was about helping Christians offer a progressive witness in response to social injustices, selecting one area of focus often made for hard conversations. Should we encourage people to pursue the cause about which they were the most passionate? Or should we focus on just one or two things that elicited energy (and hopefully some funding) in order to make a real impact? While I was at PCU, we mainly concentrated on racism as expressed in the criminal justice system, as well as racism in environmental pollution and degradation. In earlier years, PCU had done substantial work for LGBT rights, but that funding had dried up and those programs had shifted to other groups. For a staff of two fulltime people, some part-time administrative help, and a couple dozen core volunteers, that felt like the most we could do. Frankly, even then we were spread a bit thin. We would support other groups' events, mention and promote them, and sometimes even show up as co-sponsors on issues that were outside our focus but still within the general progressive constellation. We would often sign on to letters advocating for some policy position when colleagues requested it. But by and large that was it.

Still, I remember a phone call I received during a fundraising drive. On the urging of the board, I had recently made a number of phone calls to supporters who had given over the years. I had left messages with most, telling them what we were up to and inviting them to donate, especially if they hadn't for several years. One older gentleman took the time to call me back and told me in no uncertain terms that he had no intention of giving us another dollar unless we were more out front for Palestinian rights. On a personal level, Palestinian rights and especially the plight of Palestinian Christians is something that is very close to my heart. I have visited Israel and the Occupied Territories and heard from Israeli and Palestinian activists working against the occupation and separation wall. I had even applied through my denomination after seminary to be a mission intern to help document human rights abuses with B'Tselem, an Israeli organization. There wasn't enough funding at the time, and I eventually wound up in California instead. All this is to say that I care a lot about the issue. But what this gentleman was demanding was pretty out there. I asked him what exactly he wanted us to do? He wanted us to create and put ads in major newspapers condemning the occupation. A little annoyed, I suggested that if he donated $5,000 to help with such ads, then maybe we could do that. At that point he said he had to go and hung up. We did not receive the five grand.

Our social justice passions are a bit like our great loves. You can explain or rationalize them after the fact, but you can't necessarily predict them or fully account for them. Yes, there is some accounting: our social justice passions have to do with what we feel is closest to us, physically or emotionally. If your son or neighbor's son is wrongfully imprisoned and you have a good relationship with him, it is no surprise that you may dedicate yourself to better funding of public defenders to help accused persons receive fair trials. If your wife or neighbor is undocumented with two American-born children, you will likely focus your attention on expanding access to legalization routes—first for her, and then possibly for others like her as well.

In this sense, social justice issues choose us. I find there's not much point in trying to convince people to get engaged in one issue or another. Those who are ready to engage just need some guidance on what to do. Those who are "interested in learning more" almost never take up any specific actions. After all, there are a million potential things on which to spend your attention. If you work on this project, there are fewer hours in the week to work on another. Few, if any, social justice pitches explain why someone should dedicate their time to *this* issue instead of *that* issue, both of which seem equally valid from an ethical perspective. It makes sense. If someone is ready to move, you just need to point them in the right direction. If not, heaven and hell can't move them to act.

We have all experienced this. There are many issues that I care about, some more than others. For some, I care enough to do organizing on them. For others, I am willing to show up to others' events. And there are a few for which I won't do anything besides sign a petition or post something online. That's how the world is: I can't imagine someone who is trying to do *everything* being successful at anything. Still, it's a struggle to select only one cause. Consequently, our social justice involvement is often like serial monogamy—focus all of our energies for six months on one topic, see some progress, and then direct our energies to something else for a year. Admittedly, this partially reflects the burden of more privileged persons who are not bombarded with one particular injustice day after day, say that of inadequate housing or ICE sweeps in their neighborhood. It makes it harder to stay connected when there are so many issues that affect us only indirectly where we are asked to be in solidarity. The danger, of course, is in being a "fair-weather" activist, not staying with it for the long haul. It is easy for peripheral activists to demobilize.

Liberating Religion

Just as this is a book about social justice, it is also a book about religion. Thanks in part to the American imagination's captivity to white Evangelicalism when hearing the word "religion," some readers may feel that religion is antithetical to social justice. But many activists with a spiritual side (or spiritualists with an activist side!) cannot separate the two. Social justice and religion are two sides of the same coin. If you are currently skeptical about this point, I don't blame you. Often, religion *itself* needs to be liberated—from drawing us *away* from earthly concerns to, instead, drawing us *to* them. You may have often heard it said that following Christ is about private belief—about whether and how we "believe in God" or "believe in Jesus Christ"—and our intellectual assent to certain ideas such as that God is real, that Jesus is God, and that such beliefs are prerequisites for our salvation. Personal commitment and decision are *part* of the story, but faithfulness doesn't begin and end with what we feel in our hearts. It is also about engaging in the transformation of the world.

I care much more about how people are living out the good news than about explicating Jesus's relationship to God and the state of my eternal soul. What matters to me is that Jesus reveals a different way of living in the world, driven by a vision of society in which all people have life and have it abundantly (Jn. 10:10).

Over the years, quite a variety of theologians and activists have prioritized Jesus's vision of a transformed world filled with justice and peace. People of faith have led the abolitionist movement, pushed for child labor laws, and connected caring for creation and environmental degradation. This is what faithfulness is all about. It is more about *orthopraxy,* which means "right acting," than about *orthodoxy,* which means "right beliefs." Discipleship demands a response from us in our lives together concerning how we can better live them out for the sake of each other.

There are many biblical images that describe a future time or place in which God's will is done. Sometimes it's called the "promised land"; or, "the mountain of the Lord," to which all nations shall stream; or, "the city of God," where the waters of life flow forever from the throne of God. The most famous image in the Christian tradition is the "kingdom of God." Unlike the kingdoms of this world that rule by the logic of domination, the kingdom of God (or "divine commonwealth," as I like to call it for our non-monarchial ears) is for the dispossessed. It is akin to weeds growing in a stately garden for the sake of the birds of the air to have a home. This divine commonwealth is a place for the lost and the left out. It is where the first shall be last and the last shall be first (Mt. 20:16). It is a time where those on the bottom of their society are treated with the greatest respect, and God's preference for those crushed by oppression is embodied throughout the land. Now, as then, God judges a society by how it treats the least-well-off. This is a standard that we never fully reach. Most political compromises come at great cost, putting the least-well-off consistently last in line in attention. Those who are situationally homeless are helped before those who are chronically homeless. Those who need just a little assistance to be okay almost always come before those who would require far more resources for an uncertain result. This is economical thinking otherwise known as "getting the most bang for your buck." For example, if it takes $100 in resources to help ten people who are moderately struggling, but it takes $1,000 to help a single person in great need, most people will go with helping the ten at the lesser dollar amount. Of course, this logic consistently ignores the least-well-off. Unlike in a certain parable that Jesus told, it protects the 99 sheep but leaves behind the one that is lost and fending for itself (Lk. 15:1–7).

Additionally, efforts at social change work their ways in increments, typically gaining the most for those who are closest to adhering to mainstream society's mores and sensibilities. You can see this with LGBT rights having their biggest expansion around marriage equality. More socially ostracized persons do not immediately benefit from these expansions. They are told to wait their turn. But there always seems to be someone else who gets public support first. For economic reasons and others, we tend to practice the opposite of Kingdom priorities.

There are many different ways to discuss this vision. The Israelite prophet Micah described living under your own vine and fig tree and none making you afraid (Micah 4:4). Others talk about living in balance with nature and each other. From the angle of wealth inequality, I'm taken in by the desire for economic democracy, in which you have an equal say in your economic and your political life. Most call this democratic socialism. I'm quite happy to work toward that divine commonwealth alongside people of other faiths and secular people of conscience. I myself am motivated by Jesus's example and interpret others through that experience, but if someone else interprets my actions through their tradition and wants to work with me, I'm all for it. We need each other and are strengthened by collaborating together.

When I try to envision what "the wolf living with the lamb" equivalent would be for us today, I imagine:

- Our natural environment being a healthy one for communities across generations
- Work having dignity, with those most impacted by choices being involved in that decision-making, and poverty being abolished
- Governments not persecuting their constituents, and an end to state violence against oppressed groups and minorities
- People affirming the differences between us as a source of strength, not weakness
- Past injustices being given their proper acknowledgment and proportionate recompense
- The end of the structural "isms" of this world, and talking through remaining person-to-person grievances

I don't envision a utopia. We would still see problems. People would quarrel. Miscommunication would happen. Trust would be earned and betrayed at times. But the big-picture, macro situation would be one that by and large would be resolved. Whether or not we bring about such a divine commonwealth or kingdom of God is less my concern. What matters more to me is the journey. For that journey, we will need to free ourselves of things that whisper to us that things only move in one direction: better and better. We need to free ourselves of such lies. One big lie is called the "American Dream."

In the Grip of the American Dream

One of the biggest psychological obstacles to facing the challenges before us is what is called the "American Dream." There are differences of opinion about what the American Dream actually is. Some people say it is owning your own house, complete with a white picket fence.

Others say it's having enough money to put your kids through college and eventually retire. But while I think that these are partially correct, they miss the main thrust. If condos become the primary means of home ownership, there won't be picket fences. Does that mean the American Dream will have ended? Of course not! It just would have been applied differently. The heart of the American Dream is that your children will be "better off" than you are.

The pursuit of that dream may mean the deferral of certain benefits now. Pursuing it might mean working long hours and struggling to make ends meet with the conviction that if one works hard, plays by the rules, and has faith, the dream will come true. This is a faith in an uneven but, ultimately, upwardly moving trajectory. I have no doubt it has helped many people keep on keeping on when they might otherwise have given up. There are plenty of honorable examples of families who sacrifice so that their children can have a better future, and sometimes those sacrifices bear fruit. There is nothing inherently wrong with wanting a better future for one's kids. But increasingly, we are seeing that more and more of us are falling behind rather than getting ahead. Working hard and playing by the rules is no guarantee for success.

For example, mainstream economists have calculated what so many of us know intuitively: the average American is not financially better off than they were a generation ago. It would be one thing if both household incomes and expenses were flat. At least then we would be holding steady. But that is not the case. For over a generation, wages have essentially been flat after taking into account inflation, but costs such as health insurance, college tuitions, and rent have been rising far faster than wages. The result is that, on average, things are harder for the current generation than they were for their parents. Break things down more closely, and we see that those without college degrees are actually worse off in terms of wages. In such a scenario as ours, the only thing that keeps the American Dream alive is faith.

I use the term "faith" deliberately here, for the American Dream is indeed a trust in gradual progress across generations. But how does that square with the experience that some things are actually getting worse? Let's look at some more evidence. Voting rights enforcement for Black Americans is by all accounts worse now than it was 30 years ago, thanks to the Supreme Court's decision to undo part of the Voting Rights Act. Supporters of the change said, in effect, "America is less racist now than it was in the 1960s, so such an enforcement mechanism is no longer necessary." Following the lead of Supreme Court Justice Ruth Bader Ginsburg, others retorted, in essence, "While you may not be getting wet while it's raining because you have an umbrella over your head, that's no excuse to throw away the umbrella." Sure enough, almost immediately upon its rescission, many states started placing voting restrictions that disproportionately place a burden on Black citizens. Racism didn't magically diminish over time, little by little. It shifted. Only those blinded by an uncritical faith in progress were surprised.

It is irresponsible to say the same thing over and over again despite the evidence to the contrary. But it is not necessarily surprising. Such a stance stems from some form of fundamentalism. For many people, even those personally impacted by dislocations and disillusionment, questioning the American Dream is literally unthinkable. It is a bridge too far. What else can explain this pushback, except for some faith commitment in the idea of "America"? The tension between our faith in the American Dream and the reality we are experiencing must inevitably lead to a crisis point. Call it a crisis of faith if you will. How long till we reach the tipping point? Perhaps, a very long time. In the face of stress and uncertainty, it is not uncommon for people to gravitate toward assurances and promises, even unlikely ones— because, without them, all that many have left is despair.

How long can one assert that things are getting better, slowly but surely, when indicators show they are not? Such statements of victorious faith, whether made in a religious key or through secular Americanism, become blinders to reality. At its best, faith should complement our experience of the world rather than fly in the face of it. Tragically, we often have warped interpretations of what is happening around us, shaped by confirmation biases and ideological commitments. We may celebrate as beneficiaries of divine providence the one out of a hundred who beat the odds, or the Horatio Algers who seem to pull themselves up by their own bootstraps. If we do so, we have to admit that we are also implicitly saying to the other 99 who didn't succeed that they deserved their fate, or that it was "God's will." Perhaps they lacked moral character or didn't try hard enough. Perhaps they needed to learn how to be entrepreneurs. But most people do not want to follow that claim to its logical conclusion. They are right to be wary. It takes a hardened heart to be so cold. However, they hold back from taking the next step by claiming that the one out of a hundred who did succeed did so through luck (or theft) rather than divine action. Yes, the Divine works in the world, but not in a way that guarantees success or failure for either individuals or nations. We need to be consistent in these claims. As we will see later in this book, there are costs to such consistency, but they are worth it to help make better sense of our world.

Can't Seem to Catch a Break

If you are engaged in social justice in one form or another, I have some news for you: it is no fun being a progressive in the United States today. On multiple fronts, we feel that we are losing ground. Either issues are getting worse, or at best they are stuck in neutral. Certainly we often feel that the *needs* far outstrip our ability to address them. It's like the Titanic is sinking and our only bailing tools are little plastic pails to scoop out the rushing water.

On multiple fronts, whether of welcoming strangers, protecting the environment for future generations, strengthening democratic decision-making, turning back racism and white supremacy, or many more issues, we are not making the progress our world desperately needs. My dad always said that things are like a pendulum. They swing one way, overextend, and then there is a reaction, with the pendulum swinging back the other way. Basically, things move in cycles, even if not always evenly. Rather than society moving along in a straight line, it moves more like a wave, with highs and lows, or even as a circle that repeats itself. There are many traditions that describe such a vision: the book of Ecclesiastes says that there is nothing new under the sun (1:9). Been there; done that; we'll see this again. The Chinese classic novel *Three Kingdoms* opens with this observation: "The empire, long divided, must unite; long united, must divide. Thus it has ever been."[1] You may feel as if you are in the midst of a great historic struggle, but you are actually part of a pattern that has been repeating itself since time immemorial.

However, if things move in cycles, why have some forms of oppression shown no signs of ending? The United States has been oppressing Black people for four hundred years—this cycle hasn't changed. Industrialized countries have been destroying the planet as a habitable place through pollution and carbon emissions for two hundred years in the name of progress—that cycle hasn't changed. Men have been oppressing women for at least five thousand, if not ten thousand, years since the advent of agriculture and the rise of cities. Those are awfully long timescales to counsel patience and wait for a cycle to correct itself.

Many of us hold on to the hope that things will get better, someday, even if the struggle is long and the road is hard. As Dr. Martin Luther King Jr. said, quoting the 19th-century thinker and abolitionist Theodore Parker: "The arc of the moral universe is long, but it bends towards justice." Coming from that era, it's an idea that may even be tinged with a hint of Manifest Destiny, as Americans strode across the continent, and there was rapid technological and economic progress. America was on the rise, and if you were a white man, progress surely seemed inevitable, even if it was delayed. Of course, if you were a victim of American expansion as an indigenous community, or enslaved as an African American, such "progress" was at your expense.

Whether or not we agree with the imagery King reappropriated for his era, the question nagging me is this: *How long?* How long is such a moral arc? Is it one generation, two generations, or maybe ten generations? Also, is there only one moral arc? Could there be multiple arcs? Isn't it more accurate to say that, as some things improve, others actually become worse? Nonetheless, in numerous ways, life is better

---

[1]Luo Guanzhong, *Three Kingdoms,* trans. Moss Roberts (Berkeley and Los Angeles: University of California Press, 2014), 5.

than it was two hundred years ago. Life expectancy is way up. Literacy rates have increased, too. Multiple diseases, once fatal, have been wiped out (so long as we maintain vaccination rates). Black Americans won their civil rights and formal *de jure* segregation has ended. On the other hand, military actions have increased in duration and, once initiated, they seldom end. Soon enough, there will be American soldiers in Afghanistan who were born during that conflict. Such wars may be "low-grade" (from an American perspective) and involve relatively few American casualties, yet neither the victims of drones and bombings nor their families in places such as Syria, Afghanistan, or Yemen would say that things are getting better. Income and wealth inequality are at their worst point in the U.S. in nearly a century, exacerbating unequal opportunities between races. The trajectory of the current arc is toward even greater disparities, and I see no internal mechanisms to change that trajectory.

Can future generations turn things around? Oppression can seem interminable, but this doesn't preclude a future change in practices. For instance, resolving an issue, such as raising the minimum wage to a more "livable" level can be corrected years from now if it doesn't happen immediately. That does not mean we should do nothing, for otherwise in the intervening years many people will suffer and struggle to get by.

That same long-term timeline hurts us in other areas. Current and past decisions about climate change, for example, ripple across centuries. Even if we take all the right policy actions and achieve an economy that is more or less 100 percent free of fossil fuels, it is possible to accomplish this enormous feat too late. It matters greatly whether that task is accomplished by 2070, 2050, or 2030. With greenhouse gases such as carbon dioxide persisting in the atmosphere for hundreds, if not thousands, of years after being released, there *is* such a thing as too little, too late. Such a catastrophe would indeed result in "visiting the iniquity of the parents / upon the children / to the third and the fourth generation" (Num. 14:18) and far beyond.

So, I imagine you asking, "What's the point of doing anything if it's all for naught? If we are going to lose, why should we even try?" It's certainly true that many religious people have grounded their faith and activism in the biblical promise that someday, somehow, God will set things right on the earth. After all, that is the instinct of the book of Revelation. In popular culture, Revelation is about judgment, fire from the sky, being "left behind," and the end of the world. Yet actually the key claim of that most-misunderstood final book of the Bible is that the problems of our world are so big that eventually Jesus is going to have to return and set things right. In doing so he will usher in the kingdom of God on earth, where justice and peace will reign forever. This was a promise of hope for communities that were struggling and dying under Roman imperial power. It's been a source of comfort to many oppressed people ever since.

Most oppressed people, most of the time, look to a future promise of a guaranteed victory in order to help themselves survive. For those of us who are religious, our language emphasizes God's sovereignty. We say that weeping may stay for the night, but joy comes in the morning (Ps. 30:5). We say that we may be enslaved by Pharaoh, but God will lead us out of Egypt and into the promised land. I am not opposed to such notions per se. There is much to affirm about them, and I regularly use them in my own preaching and teaching. If one means by them that evil never has the final victory—that there will always be another day on which faithfulness can be expressed—then I'm all for it. If it means that God has not forgotten us but sees our troubles, and desires a better future for us, I'm all in. But if it means that good always triumphs over evil, hold the phone—I'm out. The problem is when we imply that a future of justice is *guaranteed.*

When the future is guaranteed and God is going to solve these problems, then why on earth hasn't it already happened? Trying to justify this delayed victory is how so many pastors and theologians get bogged down. One Black theologian, William R. Jones, clearly saw the contradiction between the promises of God's liberation and the ongoing predicament of Black oppression. He asked a question that 40 years later still has not been satisfactorily answered by those who hold to a more traditional understanding of God's power: *Is God a White Racist?* Meaning, if God has the power, why haven't Black people been liberated yet? If they haven't been liberated yet, maybe God isn't on the side of Black liberation. William R. Jones wanted the Black church and theologians to wrestle with this dilemma. Jones's question—and many others like it—is one that we still need to address.

It Doesn't Have to Be This Way

To resist social evil, we hold onto the courageous hope that our world *can* be more just and less oppressive even while being clear-sighted about how difficult this *will* be. After all, the future is partially dependent on how we act and respond to the challenges before us. If we respond faithfully, there is a better chance that a more just world will be realized.

The other option highlights fate, the inevitability of victory. But if the victory is inevitable, whether we envision the kingdom of God, stateless communism, or a just and regulated capitalism with a strong Scandinavian-style social safety net as our utopia, why work for it? Arguments about guaranteed ends or fate inevitably clash with a need to motivate us to do the actual work. If it all works out in the end, why not just take an economic "free ride" and receive all the benefits of victory without any of the costs or sacrifices necessary to get there? Or, perhaps even more ethically troubling, it is easier to justify sacrificing the wellbeing of some people if the end result is guaranteed and going to be so amazing: the "You've got to break some eggs to make an omelet of peace and justice" cop-out. From that line of thinking, isn't it more compassionate to let some people suffer now if it helps us achieve a paradise for many people later? These are not simply theoretical debates. Millions have perished in the name of someone else's "soon-to-be-realized utopia."

Take homelessness. It is increasing rapidly in cities across the country as rents spike and mortgages remain out of reach for many people. Some people suggest less regulation and more market-based pricing as the solution. The idea is that, over the long run, more units will be available and the price will stabilize. If people lose their homes or are forced out of apartments as rents skyrocket on the way to a better housing market, so be it, they say. Such market fundamentalists remain viscerally opposed to responses such as rent controls or affordable housing mandates. The present sacrifices of people and their immediate housing needs are worth it, they say, for a yet-to-be-realized housing utopia. Yet, even among progressive activists who show concern for the needs of the least of these, we still see such sacrificial logic in the service of a different utopia. But if our goals are less inevitable, we are also less prone to take actions that devalue the lives of others. The way we journey to our destination becomes as important as where we are trying to go.

These are large problems that for generations have bedeviled activists and those who dream of a more just world. No one book can pretend to solve all these issues. But if we ask better questions of ourselves, we can offer a better chance at a more just future. Such questions include: How should we understand power, both ours and God's, in the face of injustice? If evil often wins, how can we faithfully respond in hope of a better day? How have people endured across generations, and how can we learn from them today? If we can give compelling answers to these questions, then we just might have a shot at a better future after all.

"What Kind of Activist Are You?" Quiz

INSTRUCTIONS: Answer each question by marking A, B, or C. After completing the quiz, add 0 points for each A answer, 1 point for each B answer, and 2 points for each C answer.

1. How varied are the types of issues for which you will come out?
    A. One. I've got my thing and I'm set.
    B. A few. You've got to show up when other people need you.
    C. Many. LGBT rights, immigration rally, homeless advocacy, climate change? I'm there!

2. How far are you willing to travel for an action or event?
    A. Less than 5 miles. Why travel? The problem's right here.
    B. Up to 30 miles. We're a region and we've got to stick up for each other.
    C. Over 200 miles. We're hitting the road and building a movement!

3. Think of the last issue in which you were active. Why did you become involved?
    A. When your family's dying, you ain't got a choice.
    B. I heard a story from a friend and was moved to respond.
    C. I read about it online and was pissed off.

4. When you go to an action, what do you hope to gain?
    A. If you're not organizing and building power, I don't know why you're there.
    B. Expressing our values and being a witness for justice.
    C. The emotional high by being with like-minded people for a cause.

5. What's your favorite protest chant to lead or say?
    A. Whose streets? Our streets!
    B. Show me what democracy looks like. This is what democracy looks like!
    C. The whole world is watching! The whole world is watching!

6. On any justice issue, what has been your longest period of commitment?
    A. Five years or more. The system doesn't give up so neither shall we.
    B. One year or more. Campaigns take follow through.
    C. One month, give or take. I was there, I showed up, and I'm off to the next one.

7. How many within your closest circle are involved in your activism?
    A. Basically everyone. We live, eat, and breathe this stuff.
    B. My significant other and/or best friend (when I drag them along).
    C. Friends see it on my Facebook feed. Does that count?

Scoring:

0–3   *You are a front-line, directly affected activist. Others may come and go, but you are in it for the long haul.*

4–6   *You are driven as a progressive ally, with some issues having a more personal impact.*

7–9   *The idea of justice motivates you, and being active is as much about expressing your values and character as about the issues themselves.*

11–14   *Either you are leading a nationwide, multi-front organization, or you're all over the place!*

CHAPTER 1 DISCUSSION QUESTIONS

- In what forms of activism are you involved? What brought you to an issue originally?

- What has kept you engaged in your activism? Conversely, what has sapped your interest?

- When have you seen the American Dream to be an illusion? Why do people resist questioning it?

- When have you had an experience of feeling confident that justice would prevail only to see the reverse occur? What did it feel like, and how did you respond?

- What do you hope to gain from this book?

For Further Reading

Alexander, Michelle. *The New Jim Crow: Mass Incarceration in the Age of Colorblindness*. Revised Edition. New York: New Press, 2012.

Coleman, Monica A. *Making a Way Out of No Way: A Womanist Theology*. Minneapolis : Fortress Press, 2008.

Jones, William R. *Is God a White Racist?: A Preamble to Black Theology*. 1973. Reprint. Boston: Beacon Press, 1998.

Rieger, Joerg. *Christ and Empire: From Paul to Postcolonial Times*. Minneapolis: Fortress Press, 2007.

Sölle, Dorothee. *Thinking About God: An Introduction to Theology*. Translated by John Bowden. London: SCM Press, 1990.

2

Hoping to Make the Impossible Possible

While in seminary, I wound up as the chair of the social justice committee. Part of my job was to help students find ways to become more engaged in social justice activism. While we worked mainly on campus and local issues, sometimes we took on projects from a broader perspective. Through a former college professor, I had learned about the School of the Americas (SOA) located at Fort Benning in Columbus, Georgia. It was the place where the U.S. trained paramilitary forces from Central America in counterrevolutionary tactics. Some of those same trainees were responsible for a number of massacres in villages as well as assassinations of Catholic priests and nuns. For over a decade, there had been an annual protest and civil disobedience action outside the fort commemorating the martyrdom of these Catholic workers and seeking to shut down the School of the Americas.

In 2006, there was persistent chatter from various sources that this was the year that the School of the Americas might actually be closed. It had changed its name a few years before that to the Western

Hemisphere Institute for Security Cooperation, yet without any substantive changes in its work. There was a military authorization bill up for a congressional vote, and there were significant attempts to include defunding the SOA in that bill. A few colleagues told me there was a real chance to close down the institute permanently, and it really mattered how many people showed up for the protest.

I convinced several seminarians to take a weekend drive from St. Louis, Missouri, to Fort Benning for the event. We made arrangements to stay overnight at a nearby church. Once we arrived, we made camp, and early the following morning we went to the site of the protest and vigil. As we surveyed the different groups there, we were impressed by the variety and creativity of expression. I, for one, had never seen large puppets carried on people's shoulders. Apparently it is a popular resistance tool in parts of Latin America. One of the seminarians decided to volunteer to be a puppeteer for a pageant that afternoon, playing the role of a dictator-general. He put on a harness that fit over his back and shoulders, with the puppet rising easily an additional six feet above him. In each of his hands was a pole that attached itself to the puppet's hands. All he had to do was move the poles to make the puppet's hands move. His face would eventually be hidden with a permeable mesh material that went over his body, hiding the human beneath the puppet. His face and chest were hidden behind the puppet's torso.

Along with practicing for the pageant with other volunteers, we observed the various festivities. That afternoon, we all participated in the vigil, nearly twenty thousand activists in total. In the crowd of people, each of us was seemingly a drop in an endless ocean of activists. We each raised a handheld cross with the name of an individual killed by someone trained at the SOA. Through a loudspeaker, names of those who had been assassinated or massacred were listed. After each name the crowd roared, "¡Presente!" This went on for perhaps an hour, with the throng slowly filing past the closed chain link gate of the fort's main entrance. When I arrived at the closed gate, I saw thousands of crosses already on the gate and added mine.

It was a moving experience; it was a spiritual experience; it was one the seminarians and I talked about for much of the eight-hour drive back to the seminary campus. Yet, more than a decade later, the School of the Americas remains open.

On to the Next Fight

For reasons that are hard to explain, I'm a sucker for seemingly lost causes and underdogs. Several organizations at which I've worked have been on the verge of closing or undergoing a major restructuring. Though some of the issues are quite unpopular, I'm drawn, for example, to ending the death penalty, opposing the use of military force, dismantling *Pax Americana,* and other issues that are not on most people's radar.

When marriage equality was achieved nationwide in 2015, a few dozen church members and I gathered at a busy intersection and interstate overpass. It was a festive celebration, with us holding signs, waving to honking cars, and taking pictures. It was fun to celebrate a hard-fought victory that had been in the works since at least 2008 with California's Proposition 8, if not the 1970s with the rise of the gay rights movement. Within the month, though, many of us were critiquing what was still missing for queer communities. Yes, marriage equality was achieved, but many queer people were still too poor to afford a home, were being attacked by the police, or were being discriminated against for their gender identity. Taking time to celebrate and be refreshed was necessary before diving back into the fray.

Most activists are rarely satisfied with things as they are, even after they have won a major victory. While a passive supporter may feel joy in seeing how far our society moves forward in an area, the activist feels the distance between where we are and where we need to be. To the extent that where we need to be is a utopian vision, such as the kingdom of God or a classless society free of violence, disappointment is a perpetual stance and therefore many activists have a hard time celebrating victories for long. Over the years, the most I have been able to manage is to take a week (sometimes only a day) to celebrate a justice win such as a wage increase for workers, a clean power regulation, or the protection of a formerly persecuted group. After that, I feel the need to keep pressing for whatever's needed next. It's the mindset of the group "Sweet Honey in the Rock," who sing: "*We who believe in freedom shall not rest until it comes.*" Well, it's not here yet, and resting on our laurels won't make it happen anytime sooner!

There is a lot of value to feeling this way, particularly given the intersectional nature of injustice. What I mean by this is that most injustices are interconnected. Take marriage equality. We achieved that goal, while more couples (queer and straight) are now avoiding marriage altogether because of the economic burdens they are experiencing. They simply don't feel like they can afford to get married without more financial stability. The result is that marriage is becoming increasingly a life achievement of the upwardly mobile. Is that a step forward? Perhaps, but it is surely a halting step. When visiting Argentina for a 2013 conference, I learned about the broad coalition there that had fought against the Catholic Church and others for marriage equality. After their victory, which had also included state funds for gender reassignment surgeries, the coalition said, "Yes, it's great that we have marriage equality, but what about protecting indigenous rights?" Indigenous communities had supported the broader marriage movement, and now the respective activist groups were supporting them in their struggle. That is a faithful approach to an intersectional struggle of solidarity, and an example of how activists can support interrelated struggles after achieving victories for those issues closest to their hearts.

Tilting at Windmills

The mission to which you are called is where your passion aligns with a great need. If you are passionate about something but there is no felt need, it might be a significant hobby for you, or something you want to learn more about, but it won't be a mission. Alternatively, you may find that there is a need that you are completely unprepared to address and to which you do not have any energy to give. Of course, our passions can change. I did not always care about mass criminalization, for instance. Sure, I was vaguely aware of anecdotal instances of police harassment of people I knew, but I had not looked at the issue in any depth, nor did I understand just how systemic a problem it is. Besides, there were other things I was working on, like trying to end the Iraq War and pushing for humane immigration reform. (At the time, it didn't occur to me that hatred against immigrants and over-incarceration are connected.) However, as I met more people who had been affected by incarceration and police violence, talked with other activists working on this issue, and read Michelle Alexander's book *The New Jim Crow*, my previous passion for anti-racism work found a new home in fighting mass criminalization. In short, our passions can grow from previous passions. It is probably better to find an actual need about which you are not yet passionate and become invested in its resolution than trying to create a need for something about which you are already passionate. The latter, of course, is not impossible: sometimes needs are unnamed until some passionate person or group gives voice to them. The birth of the environmental movement in the 1960s is such an example.

There are other ways to configure great needs and our passions. You might argue that we should put our energy exclusively where we can make the biggest difference. We might call this the low-hanging fruit option. There might be a bigger problem, such as spatial segregation in cities through the legacy of race-based discrimination, which now lives on through "good schools" and high property values. But we decide that we can more easily push for local police reforms on where they patrol and to halt profiling in neighborhoods predominantly home to persons of color. Not that the latter is easy! But it is easier than reforming the way we organize our cities around wealth and exclusivity. A church may focus on helping a dozen people in a rotating winter shelter program find permanent housing to provide some stability to their lives instead of pushing the city government to offer affordable housing units throughout their town. The former is not the biggest problem we face, but it is one in which people may feel they can make a real difference with the time and resources they have to offer.

What if we pursue the alternative option and go after the biggest problem? From a personal financial perspective, this would be like focusing on paying off the largest of our credit card debts, specifically the one with the highest interest rate. That would improve your financial situation the most. But we humans do not always act rationally. We crave rewards and the feeling of accomplishment. So, financial gurus often recommend paying off the *smallest* debt first in order to have a sense of accomplishment and motivation so one does not give up. Applied to issues of social justice, if we focus on the biggest problem we can identify, it might be a five-to-ten-year struggle, one in which we see few victories along the way. Won't most people flag in zeal in the meantime? This is why community-organizing groups often start not with the biggest problem in a community, but the one in which they can find a win and be energized for the next fight. It's called "building power." People want to be part of something that has a sense of forward momentum.

For me, the issues about which I care the most tend to focus around injustices connecting race, class, and planet, and movements that use nonviolent direct action to accomplish their objectives. If a justice issue is outside that framework, I might be an occasional supporter. I might cheer you on, or attend a specific action if a friend personally invites me. I may go because it's important for the sake of our relationship that I be there, but those other areas aren't my particular passions. Addressing racism is. Challenging classism is. Protecting people and the planet from climate chaos and exploiting the earth for profit is. But these are huge issues. So, in practice that means that I try to find more local efforts that are fighting for *this change,* for *that policy* that has a better chance of winning in the near-to-midterm future. I yearn for a future with 100 percent fossil-free energy, but in the meantime I have supported community efforts to restrict oil drilling to no closer than 2,500 feet from homes in the Los Angeles area, which would in practice reduce those drilling sites by over half. It's a hard effort, but it aligns with my commitments to the extent that those who are poor, working class, and people of color are disproportionately affected by urban oil drilling.

The question that haunts most of us who feel similarly is the Don Quixote dilemma: Should we tilt at windmills, however unlikely their fall, or should we focus on purely achievable, incremental wins? If I know

> *I'm a sucker for seemingly lost causes and underdogs.*

ten thousand people are going to a rally, part of me asks, "Do they really need me there?" I want to attend things where my presence makes a difference. I'm more inclined to go to a smaller event outside a mosque supporting Muslims on inauguration day with 50 allies. So, when I think about the things about which I'm the most passionate, it's issues that seem most intractable. In a country that is politically polarized and in which many voices lament our inability to work together "across the aisle," my instinct is different. I'm suspicious of bipartisan actions for good reason. We should distrust the dominant consensus around our country. Instead of wanting to grow our economy forever, we need an economy that meets needs rather than perpetually expands desires. Instead of maintaining our military dominance, we need to work toward demilitarization. Instead of reflexive support of government actions in Israel, we need to hear what Palestinians are worried about. Instead of maintaining U.S. dominance in service of financial capital, we need to move to a more democratic, collaborative model of international relations. Each of these violates some bipartisan consensus. That makes the job an uphill, windmill-tilting struggle for sure.

A Case for Visionary Gradualism

How do we reconcile the need to fix our massive problems while also building up wins in the meantime? I'm a fan of "visionary gradualism," a term used originally by Democratic Socialists of America founder Michael Harrington to describe the transformation toward economic democracy. It is actually a helpful metaphor for a range of issues because it holds in tension revolutionary and reformist goals, but in a complementary way. Activists debate whether a specific policy change is likely to reform a system or get at the root of a problem. Often, this feels like mere semantics. We might say that passing a living wage ordinance in a city is more radical than a more modest minimum wage increase, but someone else might justifiably respond that it still involves people selling their labor in a capitalist system. A revolution in one person's eyes is a meager reform in another's. We could argue that it would be a radical shift to have mandatory body cameras on police officers and forbid police departments from withholding images to shape their preferred narrative, but another activist can justifiably say that we need police abolition and anything else is a mere patch on a bad system. Do you see the problem? The line of reform vs. radical revolution is very much in the eye of the beholder.

That's why I cling to "visionary gradualism." What do I mean by this? To be a visionary means to be captivated and driven by an image, a dream, a value, such as the "kingdom of God," or, as I call it, the divine commonwealth. While visionaries look to the world that does not yet exist, gradualism focuses on where we are right now. It looks at our world and its problems and asks, "What's the next step? What is one thing we can do that will be a measurable improvement?" It reminds us, "Don't let the perfect be the enemy of the good." This means don't let your dreams, which may or may not come to fruition, get in the way of a concrete step in the right direction. Regarding marriage equality, a gradualist might say to radicals dismissive of the extension of the right to marry to same-sex couples: "I agree that marriage is becoming increasingly reserved for a comfortable middle-class, and this does little to help homeless gay youth on the streets. Also, I agree that the queer rights movement has historically been less about fitting into a mainstream conception of family than of reconfiguring what family should be. Still, it is a step in the right direction for gay and lesbian couples to be able to marry if they wish—it's a step in the right direction."

A major critique of gradualism is that if the only change we ever focus on is incremental, then we end up abandoning demands for the big changes our world needs. Increasing car fuel efficiency from 25 to 50 miles per gallon is good, but it achieves less than we imagine if people end up driving more. This would end up offsetting much of the fossil fuel reductions. It becomes positively harmful if we think that having a fuel-efficient hybrid or plug-in car means we have done our sufficient share. It can pacify us instead of motivating us to demand an end to fossil fuel production and movement toward a 100-percent renewable energy economy.

The synthesis of these two extremes is visionary gradualism. It is more of a mindset than a precise policy prescription. It is about maintaining our radical goals and dreams based on an understanding of the root problems and what is needed to address them. At the same time, we actively support more proximate actions that are steps toward that larger vision, even though they alone will not get us there. Visionary gradualists recognize that those in power will co-opt their causes as they achieve momentum and that this is the cost of winning. They will recognize that some people will drop out of activism after their own goals are achieved regardless of whether the full work is accomplished. They will celebrate a partial victory one week, and then critique the revised system because of whom it now leaves out. They will recognize that the work is never complete, but that there are steps that can be taken in the short and midterm that will provide measurable improvements in people's lives. The vision will be revolutionary even as the action items are often reformist. The rhetoric may be fiery, but the results will be only a few degrees warmer from where we previously were. I once heard a gay activist say, "We have to demand everything now in order to get something eventually." I think this is spot on. Pure gradualists who only want to look at the next achievable step are often bereft of vision, of what our world needs, while pure visionaries can be derisive of actual lives and opportunities, loving the world in their minds more than the world as it is. Both are right *and* both miss something important. Our world needs more visionary gradualists.

Winnable Goals and Witnessing to Visions

When I was a congregation's associate pastor, I was responsible for helping to develop the social justice ministries of the church. We formed different ministry teams around issues that people cared about, and one of them was peace. At the first meeting, we went around sharing why we cared about peace and what we hoped to achieve. A number of people talked about their passion for getting the U.S. out of current military operations that were causing the deaths of thousands of civilians in Iraq.

During our brainstorming time about goals, I invited people to envision what they would like to see accomplished five years from now because of our work. One energetic lifelong activist woman chimed in, "I'd like to see the military base next to us shut down!" It was true that we were just a few miles from a major military installation. About

80 percent of my own apartment complex housed military personnel, primarily Marines. Close to one-third of the jobs in the adjacent town were directly dependent on the presence of that base. To put it mildly, there was not a snowball's chance in hell that we would shut down that base in five years, especially with the seven people we had in the room. I gently guided us back to what *we* could potentially accomplish in more incremental steps.

Maybe my response was too skeptical. Maybe I could have encouraged her vision. But overall I'm convinced that in terms of accomplishing what we want, we need winnable goals that energize us. Like any good community organization, we have to recognize what is a difficult but achievable victory and what is not. Sometimes that means we do things even if we know we won't win. Near a seminary in the Los Angeles area, there is a corner on the street where for years a number of older peace activists have planted themselves every Friday, waving signs at passing cars. They demand "Peace Now" or "Money for Schools, not Bombs," etc. What brings them back each week is as much their commitment to each other as it is a desire to see those demands met. I don't know if they really think their weekly demonstration will shift American foreign policy, but they know it may inspire others. It reminds onlookers who feel similarly that there are like-minded people out there who are doing something about it.

But which cause deserves our support? What might be an actionable issue for your activism? For those who can withstand an hour-long litany of terrible things happening in the world from a leftist perspective, the radio and online news organization "Democracy Now!" is as a good place as any to get your news. It was on a morning in May 2013 that I watched online one specific report there that motivated me to action. Amy Goodman, the host, was talking about a direct action by Guantanamo Bay detainees. They were angry about mistreatment in detention. They were despondent because many of them had been cleared for release years ago yet still languished there. They were on the verge of giving up on the idea that anything could ever be better for them. So, in their desperation, they launched a hunger fast. Already, there were concerns about our government force-feeding detainees through nasal tubes, which constitutes torture.

I was convicted. Immediately, I knew that most Americans wouldn't give a rip about what Guantanamo detainees did, fasting or otherwise. After all, doesn't our government designate most of them as terrorists? Weren't the detainees using our concern for human rights as a weakness in order to manipulate us? I myself didn't believe any of that, but I knew others who did. A feeling came over me to the effect of: "You can't do nothing." Most Americans might not care what happened to them, but I was an American citizen. Male. White. A minister. Such advantages I had been given regardless of my merits could be used for something good here. I hadn't eaten breakfast yet that morning, instead catching up on the news first. Overcome with emotion, I committed then and there to join their hunger fast.

I didn't know what I was doing, having only ever fasted for 24 hours in college. But I proceeded anyway. Finding the email address of one of the attorneys who was representing some of the detainees, I contacted them, asking whether my fasting would be something that would be useful and appreciated by his clients. With a big, "Absolutely!" I was set. Though "Democracy Now!" only airs on the weekdays, I must have been delayed in watching the Friday recording, because I later went to church that afternoon. The scripture being preached on was about Paul and Silas being in prison and of how the angel of God opened up the cells. This was a sign!

Before long, I was put in touch with half a dozen other people who had each independently committed to fasting. We shared our reasons why we were doing what we were doing and supported each other. I wrote up a petition and began circulating it, urging people to sign on, demanding that then President Obama use his executive authority to release those already administratively approved to leave. I began calling my U.S. Representative and Senators' offices each morning, informing them of my fast. Not being a particularly large person (I started the fast at 137 lbs.), I didn't know how long I would be able to do it. I committed to taking it one day at a time. On the morning of the third day, I received a call from Senator Feinstein's office. They were concerned about how long my fast was going to go on. After all, it's bad press for a senator to do nothing when a constituent is fasting and calling them every day. I told her staff that I was taking it one day at a time but I would stop tomorrow if the President announced a release schedule for those eligible.

Was the detainees' plight the most important thing happening in the world? Probably not. Almost simultaneously an even larger hunger strike was happening at the Pelican Bay prison in California. The lives of about 160 persons at Guantanamo, some of who had done terrible things, is relatively microscopic in the grand scheme of righting the world. But when faced squarely with an existential dilemma, you must make a decision. *Now.* For me, that decision led to a nine-day fast.

There were small successes. Mainly from the pressure of the detainees and news reports of forced feeding (I highly doubt my small contribution forced his hand), President Obama held a news conference concerning the Guantanamo detainees. He said nice things, but refused to commit to any measurable actions. Eventually, he was interrupted by a Code Pink activist who called him out. After the fact, he charged someone with the task of expediting the release of those eligible. Within a year from that time, the number of detainees was reduced from 165 to a little over 80. By the time he left office in 2017, less than 60 detainees remained. Of course, there were other, more problematic, reasons why the number of detainees declined. For one, no new persons were being added to the detention center. The administration had learned that housing people in Guantanamo was more trouble than it was worth, working unsuccessfully to close down the Guantanamo Bay Detention Center. But instead of apprehending suspects, the U.S. increasingly used aerial assaults with drones. Instead of being detained, suspects were simply killed. Any man aged 18-to-40 killed in a drone strike was declared a suspected militant. Their family was welcome to provide evidence to clear their names after the fact. That's a small consolation to losing a loved one. As in almost all struggles, even as some things improve, others become markedly worse. Some people win, and some people lose.

There Are Winners and There Are Losers

No one likes to lose. People definitely do not like being called "losers." We want to be winners—to have things go our way, to be seen as victorious. The terms "winners" and "losers" go hand in hand. This connection is most explicitly expressed in the language of economics. When evaluating a policy or trade deal, it is not uncommon to hear an economist say, "There will be winners and losers." As it relates to a trade deal, they mean something to the effect that many people will benefit from lower costs, but other people will lose their jobs: "winners" and "losers." To their minds, as long as the winners benefit more than the losers are hurt, it is worth it. Losers become a sacrifice for the wellbeing of winners.

The language of winners and losers is very popular in current political rhetoric. Of course, different policies are established or defeated; different politicians gain power or are thrown out. But beyond being a mere descriptive of this process, people place value on the winners and judgment on those who lose. To call someone a loser does not sound in our ears as a descriptive term; it sounds like a term of judgment and condemnation. It sounds like a moral evaluation of someone's failings. And that is exactly how it is used in the mouths of the powerful. It functions like a schoolyard taunt.

Unlike this judgmental angle that celebrates victory as good and failure as some moral lacking, I invite you to see things differently. The Bible is written from the underside of history. It is the story of peoples who travel when they are desperate, are continually occupied by foreign powers, flee from tyrants, speak and are ridiculed, cry out for justice and are killed. It is the story of losers and God's journey with them. Many of its themes do not make sense from the perspective of the powerful. For instance, "hope" has no meaning if you are winning. Hope is about not giving up when things are going terribly for you. It is about believing that things can be better, despite no obvious evidence that they will ever improve. I mean the following in the most affirming way possible: hope is for losers. As Jesus said, "Those who are well have no need of a physician, but those who are sick" (Mk. 2:17). The only thing that faith offers the winners of this world is the smug claim that they deserve what they have. Yet their assurance is more a curse than a blessing, for it blinds them to the values that bless the oppressed. Read these blessings: who are they for, winners or losers?

Blessed are you who are poor,
for yours is the kingdom of God.
Blessed are you who are hungry now,
for you will be filled.
Blessed are you who weep now,
for you will laugh.
Blessed are you when people hate you,
and when they exclude you,
revile you, and defame you
on account of the [Human One]. (Lk. 6:20–22)

These are the blessings of losers. Hope is for losers. The good news is for losers. It is the losers of this world who pray that the impossible—a world of genuine justice and peace despite the evidence—can become possible through our struggles and faithfulness. They can follow a model: one who was a great loser—who our world is all-too-quick to cloak in triumph and victory. When we look to Jesus, we see a loser *par excellence*.

Jesus: An Unlikely Example

Religious traditions try to make sense of life's ambiguous results. Still, it is odd to have a religious tradition make its central symbol out of someone who, for his time and culture, was surely considered a loser. Jesus of Nazareth did not have an especially successful life. He wandered through villages, gathering misfits, laborers, and the left out. His crew would be the most unimpressive group ever to serve on a board of directors. His family questioned his sanity (Mk. 3:21). His hometown rejected his ministry (Mk. 6:5–6). People from more prominent places, such as Jerusalem, thought of Nazareth as a religious and cultural backwater (Jn. 1:46). Indeed, his entire country was occupied by Rome and considered by its authorities as a backward frontier. Whether homeless by choice or circumstance, he had "nowhere to lay his head" (Mt. 8:20), besides being welcomed into homes as he traveled. He wrote no known treatises, and left no surviving documents or artwork. The only records of him were the stories his rag-tag group of followers shared with others after the fact.

Today, Christians read the stories in the gospels and in Paul's letters as if, back then, the whole world was hanging on his every word, as if they were asking: "What is this Jesus guy going to do next?" But back then, even as the Roman occupying authorities were having him executed for sedition, someone was sleeping in while another was buying food from the market. It was just another day for most people.

When we hear the word *crucifixion,* we Christians generally have only one of them in mind: Jesus's, the one for the sake of the world, to wash away our sins. But crucifixion was a relatively common form of capital punishment in Jesus's day, especially to stop rebellions. Started by the Persians to punish their failed generals, crucifixion was picked up by the Romans as a tool of state terrorism to beat unruly populations into psychological submission. The 1960 Stanley Kubrick movie *Spartacus* gives the sense of this, when a slave revolt is put down with a mass crucifixion along a major road. The biblical historian John Dominic Crossan argues that such events were not aberrations, and often thousands were crucified as a punishment meant to be shameful, to embarrass the one being executed and those who looked upon them. It was meant to show that this person and their efforts had come to naught.[1] Their vision for the world was as dead as them. They were a loser of the highest order. Everyone who saw them was meant to look and think, "Thank goodness that isn't me!"

Churches who display images of Jesus's death often soft-pedal aspects of it to maintain Jesus's dignity, to blunt the horror. Among the vast majority of crucifixes, paintings, and film representations, Jesus is given an undergarment to wear. But in reality, he would have been naked, exposed. His skin would have blistered. For all to see, he would have lost control of his bodily functions. He would have been unclean and disgraced, an embarrassment to all who knew him. Few followers could watch such a terrible fate. Most victims of crucifixion would not have been given a proper burial, based on the belief that

---

[1]John Dominic Crossan, *Jesus: A Revolutionary Biography* (New York: HarperCollins, 1994), 143.

their spirits would not be able to rest. Either no grave or a shallow grave would mean animals would feast on the remains. It was state terrorism. It was appalling. It was a loser's death.

It is no wonder that subsequently there were few images of the cross in churches for several centuries. Actual crosses were a symbol of terror, not worship. The closest contemporary equivalent in our day would be for a church to make a lynching noose the symbol of divine victory. We recoil at the thought. How could such a horrible event and symbol ever be turned into an inspirational image? It was in large part thanks to Constantine, who became the first Christian Emperor of Rome, that the image of the cross was reimagined as a state symbol of triumph. According to popular tradition, Constantine had a vision of a cross in the sky just before the Battle of the Milvian Bridge, a vision he took to be a symbol of his divinely approved victory. He ordered his soldiers to paint crosses on their shields and they were victorious.

We're a long way from the cross being an image of state-sponsored terrorism. It has become a symbol of state-sanctioned victory. A symbol of losers has been converted into a symbol of triumph.

As for the disciples of Jesus, they aren't particularly striking individuals in terms of their social status. These early leaders of the movement that would become Christianity were not much more successful than their leader. The Lord they proclaimed, Jesus of Nazareth, was executed for sedition. His brother and subsequent head of the Jerusalem Church, named James, according to tradition was pushed off the temple and then pummeled with rocks. The apostle Peter was crucified upside down. Paul, that crucial developer of the Christian tradition, was eventually beheaded in Rome itself. These are not the kinds of stories we tell about what it means to grow up and be a great success. Few parents encourage their children to aspire to be martyrs. So, what made Jesus so remarkable?

What Kind of Lord?

The philosopher Alfred North Whitehead once said that, regarding divine power, the Church erred when it gave unto God that which belonged exclusively to Caesar. By this, he meant that the qualities that make someone an emperor are different from what makes someone divine. Part of the problem is that the labels and titles that start as counter-culturally provocative in one context are co-opted in another context. Take, for example, the title of "Lord." This was one of the earliest, if not *the* earliest, title that the first followers gave to Jesus after his death. It was also a common title given to the Roman emperor. By saying that Jesus is Lord, Christians were also making a claim against Rome. If everything is great with your Roman lord, there is no need to proclaim another one. But Jesus's life reinterpreted for them what true lordship meant. Rather than domination and "lording" it over others, it meant service and giving yourself for others (Mt. 20:26).

These days, most of us do not have lords. The only lords with whom I interact are the feudal ones I see on the TV show *Game of Thrones*. So in our radically different setting, when people hear, "Jesus is Lord," they naturally associate that statement with more traditional notions of lords. We've turned its original meaning on its head. Instead of Jesus reinterpreting what it means to be "Lord," now "Lord" interprets who Jesus is.

Imagine what would be the most radical statement of faith challenging unjust leadership, power, and oppression in 1930s Germany. Perhaps saying, "Jesus is Führer"? There would be no need to say this if you are happy with how things are going in the Third Reich. Every German would intuitively understand such a statement to be directly challenging Nazi claims to legitimacy. But outside that context, such a phrase doesn't make sense at all. It repulses, because we instinctively interpret Jesus with the term "Führer," rather than the other way around. Instead of Jesus interpreting the mighty titles given to him, the titles wind up interpreting him.

Affirming that Jesus is the Christ has more to do with affirming the *vision* Jesus articulates than with who he is on the inside. It's less about the *person* of Jesus and more about his *priorities*. Countless debates have occurred speculating on how Jesus was able to do the amazing things he did. People who were deeply committed to Christianity mutually expelled each other from fellowship because their rationales about Jesus conflicted with each other. Such debates are irrelevant to discipleship. To affirm Jesus as Lord is just another way to say that his priorities are worth following and living for.

In responding to injustice, it's helpful to remember that God's power is made perfect in weakness. That's what Paul says in 2 Corinthians 12:9: "[God's] grace is sufficient." God's presence with us is enough. That doesn't mean we constantly have to make ourselves vulnerable to manipulation or even abuse. It doesn't mean giving up or despairing. Far from it! It's about recognizing the limitations of what we can do on our own, and how we have to rely on God to provide us with strength for the journey. When you are strong, you can forget that and think that "by my own hand" everything is accomplished. In fact, we are collaborators with God, co-conspirators. The Divine offers us options and invitations to respond faithfully to our given situation, and we do so, sometimes even surprising the source that first urged us on. But each step, no matter how tentative or incomplete, is renewed by the divine presence that invites us to "take another step." As Laozi, the ancient Chinese philosopher, once said, "The journey of a thousand miles begins with a single step." With hope undergirding each step we can take, and God's presence with us even when we grow weary, the journey goes on to make the impossible possible. That is the most faithful way to respond to injustice.

CHAPTER 2 DISCUSSION QUESTIONS

- Do you prefer emphasizing pragmatic victories or idealistic visions? To what extent do you think we can combine these faithfully?

- To what extent do you "tilt at windmills"? Are such acts a waste of our time, or do they have some other value?

- What does Paul mean when he says that power is made perfect in weakness (2 Cor. 12:9)? Do you agree with that statement? Why or why not?

- Where have you seen weakness to be a strength?

- In what ways does the cross show God's vulnerability?

- Where do you find hope in situations in which things are getting worse right now rather than better?

For Further Reading

Bonhoeffer, Dietrich. *The Cost of Discipleship*. 1937. Reprint, New York: Touchstone, 1995.

Cone, James H. *The Cross and the Lynching Tree*. Maryknoll, N.Y.: Orbis Books, 2011.

Patterson, Stephen J. *Beyond the Passion: Rethinking the Death and Life of Jesus*. Minneapolis: Fortress Press, 2004.

Sung, Jung Mo. *The Subject, Capitalism, and Religion: Horizons of Hope in Complex Societies*. New York: Palgrave Macmillan, 2011.

Thurman, Howard. *Jesus and the Disinherited*. Boston: Beacon Press, 1976.

Yoder, John Howard. *The Politics of Jesus*. 1972. Reprint, Grand Rapids, Mich.: Eerdmans, 1994.

3

Faithfulness in a World
of Suffering

At the seminary I attended, students had a field education placement each year in either a church or noncongregational setting. My first year, I served as a chaplain intern at an HIV/AIDS residential living program. I met many amazing people there, many of whom had tragic life stories. Some were struggling with addiction, while others previously had been homeless. Others had practiced unsafe sex in a world that despised them for their sexual orientation. Many were very matter of fact about their experiences; for them, life was hard and full of struggle anyway, and contracting HIV/AIDS was just one more obstacle. It's not hard to imagine an outsider walking in off the street wanting to make moral judgments about residents. Empathy was in short supply toward their lives. You could imagine the criticisms: "If you hadn't done this, if you had only done that, then perhaps you wouldn't be in this situation." Such hurtful statements are meant more for the ears of those not directly impacted by such toils and snares. People feel the need to rationalize problems and reassert a basic moral arc to the universe. Their pat answers do more wounding than healing.

For me, one person in particular put the lie to such unhelpful perspectives: Ashley. Part of my responsibilities as a chaplain there was to make rounds and visit with people who needed a friendly ear. It was in that situation that I met her. At 22, she was probably the youngest person living there. I just so happened to be the same age, so we had a natural point of reference from which to talk. Other than that, our lives were very different. Ashley had lived with HIV/AIDS for a decade ever since been sexually assaulted by a relative when she was only 12. Since that time, her health had gradually deteriorated. With little holes now opening up in her esophagus, she had reached the point where she couldn't drink or eat anything directly, lest food particles enter her lungs, so all nutrition was administered through a tube. She desperately desired to taste food and drink, so she was allowed to put them in her mouth but had to spit them out before swallowing. This was essentially an impossible condition. What is more natural than the desire to eat? Even if she could manage to avoid the desire to swallow food, some liquid or food always made its way down her esophagus along with her saliva.

When I first met her, she was already so tiny and frail. She moved like an old woman, but she talked like a typical 22-year-old who wanted to go out and live her life. It was not to be. No matter how much liquid nutrition was pumped directly into her stomach, it was never enough for her to gain any weight. She died within a year of our first meeting. When her family had a memorial service for her at the shelter, they brought with them a picture of her from when she looked healthy. Gazing at her picture—her full face, her dark skin contrasting with a bright summer dress—I wouldn't have known it was the same person.

There is no theological system in the world that can ethically justify why two 22-year-olds from similar regions of the country could have such divergent outcomes. Here I am, a cancer survivor still going strong over a decade

> *God didn't decide for me to live and Ashley to die.*

later, while Ashley has been in the ground for over a decade. Some Christians say that God does not give us more than we can handle.

Tell that to Ashley. Tell that to the thousands who die before their time. Tell that to those who are emotionally and spiritually broken by tragedy and not made stronger. Tell that to all those who give up in despair. God didn't decide that I should live and Ashley should die. God doesn't have that kind of power nor use it that way. We need to reimagine who God is in relation to evil, tragedy, and injustice. The alternative status quo is too much to bear.

Theodicy—or Why a Good God Who Could Stop Evil but Doesn't Isn't Worth Worshiping

Why do bad things happen to good people? It's a perennial question and it has to do with divine power, especially as it relates to unjust and avoidable suffering. The theological term for this is "theodicy." Specifically, what is the relationship between a good God and the terrible things that happen? People give all sorts of answers: *Is God, somehow, cool with this? Is it part of a larger plan? Is it a test? Maybe tragic events are not so bad looking back in retrospect?* People try to defend God or rationalize away evil events. They say: "God doesn't give you more than you can handle." "Everything happens for a reason." "God needed them in heaven."

All of these responses are downright hurtful or simply lackluster and insufficient. They push many people away from religion altogether. We might call such rationalizations theological malpractice. Like the Hippocratic Oath, religious answers should seek to do no harm. Not all of us directly experience profound injustice, but each of us will be confronted with death, loss, and unavoidable tragedy. Each of us at some point must wrestle with making sense of loss.

For centuries, religious thinkers have discussed the problem of theodicy. The fundamental challenge is how to reconcile three logically incompatible ideas: (1) God is totally good; (2) God is all-powerful; and (3) evil is real and not an illusion. These three ideas cannot be held together coherently. Every solution involves combining two of these items and relativizing the third. For instance, we can say that God is good and all-powerful. If that's the case, then the things we think are evil are only so from our limited human perspective. They may be part of a greater plan where the presence of apparent evil is part of some larger redemptive story. This would make evil actions worth it for the larger good they cause. But this would be dismissing evil as genuinely real. Alternatively, evil can be real and God can be all-powerful. In this case, however, God is not all good. In this option, God is both the bringer of the good and the bad, and it is our task to make sense of this. There are passages in the Bible that support this option of God being the source of both the good and the bad (Isa. 45:7), but while it's a coherent option, it is not compatible with the prophetic call for justice and liberation from evil.

Many people are tempted to have it both ways. They affirm all three ideas but then proceed to muddy the waters. The best example of this is when people argue that God creates free will in humans but has the ability to take it away. In this rendition, humans, and not God, are the cause of evil. God *could* stop the evil from happening but won't for some reason. If this is the case, that means that God again sees the evil as part of a larger good.

There is a third alternative. It is probably the least popular in American Christianity, though it does have a prevalent following among those who are inclined to what are called process, relational, and feminist theologies. In this option, we affirm that evil is real and that God is good. But it no longer sees God as all-powerful. In this option, the problem of making sense of God's relationship with evil in the world originates from a misunderstanding of what God does in the world. God's power is the power of relationship, not of coercion. God's power is the power to inspire us to do better, not to control like a divine dictator. In this option, God desires good, encourages us to resist evil, but does not have the ability to stop injustice or evil unilaterally beyond encouraging how creatures should respond. God's power has been misunderstood, leading to countless crises of faith across generations. This is the position this book most closely adopts.

All of these solutions have problems that come down to emotional resonance. Does the answer feel compelling enough that one can live with the costs? Many people find the costs of a God who cannot do certain things unworthy of their time or devotion. They ask themselves, "If God cannot stop evil from happening, why should I worship a God so conceived?" This points back to our understanding that power is revealed through weakness. What is the character of the Divine? For Christians, an additional question follows: "How is God made known through the life of Jesus?" For me, it makes far more sense to see God as one who gets crucified, laments the horrors of the world, but walks with us for a better future than as one who makes such horrors part of a larger prearranged plan.

The answer is one of logical priority or causation. We can ask it this way: Does God cause or allow evil to happen so that good can be revealed? I think we need to answer with a firm "No!" Such arguments are so repugnant that in the face of such a god, the only moral response is atheism. But we can yet affirm that, even as evil happens in our world, God responds. God invites us to confront creatively the

> *God invites us to confront creatively the horrible situations we face so that something good can come from them.*

horrible situations we face so that something good can come from them. This response doesn't make the initial injustice or evil act worth it. Of course it would have been better if that evil event had never happened. But God takes the world as it is and offers possibilities for how it can be different. If we respond, things can improve. If we don't, God will offer up another option based on the additional mess we have made.

One strength of this perspective is that it can help us understand how evil forces, systems, and powers can exist in our world and act in opposition to the Divine. This does not mean that evil is equivalent to God in power or influence. We don't need to think in terms of two warring gods, one good and one bad, perpetually fighting over the world, like the Lord of Light and his polar opposite in the TV show *Game of Thrones*. All we need to recognize is that there are forces in our world that act to destroy rather than build up value.

This summary does not resolve all issues about theodicy. There remain questions about God's culpability with evil, primarily the idea that God deems it worthwhile that a world with all its risks of failures and mistreatment exists at all—for, in order for anything valuable to exist, the option for creatures to respond negatively has to exist. In that way and that way alone can God be blamed for evil. If, on account of the reality of loss and oppression, it would have been better for nothing to have existed at all, only in that way is God guilty of allowing evil. To take that position, you have to side on a metaphysical scale with George Bailey at his lowest moment in the movie *It's a Wonderful Life*—while he wishes that *he* had never been born, we would have to say it would have been better for there to be no world at all.

Still, the natural response by many people is to reject this description of God as no God at all. If God can't do whatever God wants, some people say, that is not a God worth worshiping. Process theology answers with the opposite: that a God who could stop evil but chooses not to is the God not worth worshiping. Divine power is different from what we often see as dominating power in our world. Divine power is not a power that oppresses, exploits, or colonizes. But it does make demands on us for the sake of justice and peace in our world. When we fail, there is judgment insofar as there is an evaluation of missed opportunities, active mistreatment, and the loss of what could have been. We have to live with and be accountable for those lost chances. But there is grace in being given another opportunity to respond faithfully to what is before us.

I was given such an opportunity. When I was living through cancer, I didn't ask, "Why is this happening to me?" I took it as a given that people become sick randomly—without cause, merit, or punishment. But I did have a sense that *if* I survived, I should use the time I had to do as much good as possible. Surviving cancer at a young age, while itself a terrible event, could help me empathize with other people experiencing suffering. It could be a catalyst for good things to happen, though that did not mean that my cancer was caused in order that those good secondary responses happen. Spiritually, such an opportunity meant that God was encouraging me to use my experiences for the benefit of others for however long I might be here. As I like to say: For me, everything after cancer is "bonus time."

This dynamic is also how I see the greater struggle for social justice and a better world. The experiences we have, liberating or oppressive, do not necessarily lead to greater compassion for others. Someone could just as easily live through a similar experience and decide, "I never want to think about that again. I just want to get back to my normal life." Or, they could think, "That experience was horrible. I need to make sure that I never have to feel that again, regardless of what that might mean to anyone else. If I have to climb over someone to avoid being hurt again, so be it." It's not the events that direct our actions as much how we *interpret* and respond to them. When it comes to social injustices, the same dynamic is at work. One person sees their experiences as a chance to expand their compassion and solidarity. Another wants to push them aside and forget. Still another is willing to oppress others to achieve some sense of personal safety.

God, the Universe, or however you describe ultimate reality, gives us a lot of freedom in how we will respond to what confronts us. We cannot choose the cards we were dealt—whether they benefited us, harmed us, or were indifferent to us. But we can decide *how* we are to respond—broadening or restricting our concern—in light of those moments. We can conclude: I'll work so this never again happens to anyone, or it will never again happen to me.

We humans are meaning-making creatures. We can't help but try to make sense of what befalls us. I chose to consider receiving cancer as a blessing in disguise—not that the cancer was somehow caused in order to be a blessing. It was hell. But I realized that after it is over, it could be made into a blessing. I could take this horrible thing and find something positive from it going forward: "lemonade out of lemons." Though it can seem a bit trite, that is not too far off the mark. As a recommendation you offer to another amidst their pain, such a phrase is worse than useless. It only works as an answer you find for yourself. Even worse is, "God has a plan for you." By that, most of the time people mean God either caused or allowed the event to happen for some larger purpose. To that we should respond, "No thanks." One of the requirements in the ethics of social experimenting is the consent of the one being experimented on. The same standard would apply for God (regardless of any literary bet between God and "the Satan" in the book of Job). Discounting any divine foreknowledge, I like Joseph's statement in the book of Genesis summarizing how he interpreted his experience of being sold into slavery by his brothers: "Even though you intended to do harm to me, God intended it for good, in order to preserve a numerous people, as he is doing today" (Gen. 50:20). We can't control what happens to us, and neither can God, but even the greatest injustice can be flipped in order to produce something positive.

Social injustice and oppression are generally unmitigated disasters for people and communities. They ripple across generations, passing down traumas and pain. It would be better if they had not happened. We can pray that they will end and that justice will be done. We can work to respond to immediate problems and try to mitigate future problems. There is really only one good thing that comes out of them: they can motivate us to care for others in similar situations more deeply, to empathize with their struggles, to help them feel less alone in a seemingly uncaring world. That does not make those injustices worth it, it does not make them good things, but it does mean that good things can sometimes arise in spite of it all. Even a cross can lead to a resurrection.

The Prosperity Anti-Gospel

Unfortunately, there are many prominent voices that offer a diametrically opposed position on theodicy. While some benefit emotionally from this, a great number are doubly wounded: first from what happens to them and second by theological malpractice.

For many years now, I have tried to avoid watching televangelists on TV. They just end up making me mad. Besides, there are only so many hours in a day, so why intentionally torture myself? It would be better to go outside for a walk and enjoy creation. Still, I know that for millions of people, televangelists are some of the most influential shapers of their understanding of God and the world in which we live. In spite of the relatively recent emergence of televangelism and its massive following, it is part of a broader stream of Christian thought. By drawing upon this tradition and certain American values, such televangelists increase their earthly success and following to the detriment of many.

There is an old idea that doing well is a sign of blessing. If you are religious, you often call it a sign of God's favor. If you're secular, you say success is an indication of hard work and good character. Whether in a religious or secular setting, the result is the same: those who have wealth, status, or success assert that they deserve what they have. Those who wish they had those luxuries can idolize said figures as people to look up to and emulate. To some, they come off as obnoxious. Who wants to be around someone who assumes they are so worthy of whatever advantages they have, especially when those benefits often come from birth, luck, or outright theft? However, when you combine this pomposity with its corollary implication, they become downright dangerous. For, if the successful prosper, then what about those who are struggling? Is their struggle a sign of divine disfavor and/or lack of character and hard work?

This is how I experienced the televangelist and healer Benny Hinn. Internationally renowned for his supposed miracle-healing events, I first saw him while I was undergoing chemotherapy treatment. During his televised performance, a woman was introduced as having an illness. Whatever ailed her, it wasn't visible. Hinn then said some words, touched her forehead, and she fell back in ecstasy into the arms of two stage attendants. She arose a few moments later celebrating her healing. It didn't take long to see what was going on: no one who came up to him onstage had an impairment that was obvious to the naked eye. For example, a quadriplegic did not come up to the stage and begin walking. A man without eyes did not grow new miracle eyes. If there were any such people who wanted a blessing, TV audiences wouldn't see it. Hinn wasn't preaching a message promising comfort and divine presence. That would have been fine. He even could have spoken about spiritual healing and acceptance. That would have been great. But instead he was selling the promise of total physical healing and instant miracles via faith. "Nonsense," I thought (admittedly in more colorful language).

If Hinn had a ministry particularly devoted to the sick, I wouldn't have a problem with that. I've known many pastors and chaplains that proclaim the gospel in hospitals with great integrity. But the gospel Hinn was sharing was cruel in its implications. If you weren't healed right then and there, maybe your faith was a problem. Worse, maybe *you* were the problem. Maybe God was punishing you. It was the subtext of everything going on at his revival performances.

That alone is enough to make one's blood boil. But the thing about televangelists that specifically puts them in my theological crosshairs is the financial manipulation of vulnerable people. Can we say that God laments destitution and involuntary deprivation? That is surely a safe bet. Can we say that the divine will is for fullness and abundance of life? Sounds good to me. It's when supernatural thinking is combined with causal statements about guaranteed financial transactions and blessings that we jump into an anti-gospel of oppression.

The level of financial exploitation that occurs in so much prosperity gospel preaching is antithetical to a liberating gospel. Viewers are pressured to give monetarily to a ministry on the promise that they will receive a financial reward. At its most crass, it can sound like a too-good-to-be-true investment plan. Send $100 to this ministry and God will bless you with $200 back! If it worked, that would be a wonderful retirement plan. One of the particular violations is how those who are targeted to give are often already financially vulnerable. Either living in poverty or right on the edge, there have been instances of people sending hundreds, if not thousands, of dollars in the hopes of finding a way out of their troubles. Bishop Clarence McClendon, who has the show *Take It by Force,* encourages people to give money to the church using their credit cards. In effect, they are literally being asked to take out a high interest loan for the promise of an even higher return if they are faithful. According to *The Los Angeles Times,* McClendon has said, "Get Jesus on that credit card!" TBN, or Trinity Broadcasting Network, uses the prosperity gospel for the majority of its fundraising. There are countless examples of people giving the last of their money, sometimes in the thousands of dollars, on the deceptive promise of guaranteed returns if they only have faith. While there are always exceptions, it is safe to say that most do not receive a miraculous solution to their financial woes and are left further in poverty.

The most brazen story I heard on financial exploitation comes from the televangelist Creflo Dollar. The owner of several multi-million-dollar residences, two Rolls-Royces, and a private jet, Mr. Dollar is known for living it up thanks to the Lord's blessings. Along with Benny Hinn, Paula White, and several others, he was the focus of a Senate investigation in the 2000s on personally profiting from financial donations. The investigation was inconclusive and ended without bringing charges, but his ministries have received an "F" rating for utterly failing to be financially transparent. You may remember the story from 2014 that shocked the country. His private jet needed to be replaced, and his church started asking its membership base to raise enough to buy a new private jet at a cost of over $60 million, asking each member to give at least $300. After being ridiculed in the media, the church ended the campaign publicly—but continued it quietly without fanfare. Eventually, the church bought the fancy jet for Dollar's "ministry."

One biblical passage that might, on the surface, lend some credence to giving your very last dollar is Mark 12:41–44. Here, Jesus observes different people put money into the temple treasury. While wealthy people put in their excess, a widow puts in two copper coins. Jesus notes that she has actually given more than those donating from the excess of their abundance. Preachers point to her faith as a positive model to follow. However, the story does not explicitly affirm that what she has done is something to emulate. In fact, the passages immediately preceding and following it undermine the system in which she is swept up. In verses 38–40, Jesus condemns the elite who lord their status over others, condemning them to punishment in their efforts: "They devour widows' houses and for the sake of appearance say long prayers. They will receive the greater condemnation" (Mk. 12:40). Immediately following the widow's gift, Jesus declares that the temple will be destroyed, the very system to which she gave. So, while she may have great faith and trust in God, Jesus does not look kindly upon the institutions that are exploiting her faith even to the last two coins. Prosperity peddlers should take note.

The part that infuriates me more than anything is how televangelists will sometimes use their own lives as examples. They had nothing, and because they were faithful, look at them now. Of course they are wealthy now: they are pressuring people with religion to give them money! It requires a certain level of shamelessness to say with a straight face that if it can happen to someone with a television show, it can happen to someone in their apartment struggling to make rent. It seems that prosperity gospel leaders worship the "Almighty Dollar" more than they do the God of Jesus. The wealth that people accrue they baptize as a divine blessing rather than as a burden or even a sign of misbegotten gain. More than a trust in the God of Jesus, prosperity leaders ask people to put their faith in the perpetual accumulation of wealth. It is the divinization of capitalism in which our participation in that system becomes the means of worldly salvation.

The prosperity gospel says that health and wealth are always the will of God for us. It says that sickness and poverty can be broken by faith. You don't even have to be progressive to see this as a warped gospel; many evangelical leaders likewise condemn this gospel as idolatrous, for it understands healing as an obligation on God's end as part of the divine contract, as is the avoidance of poverty. By speaking positively about what one is owed by God, the prosperity gospel says it can be willed into existence. This positive confession gives one access to the blessings of health and wealth. You make a statement about what in your life you want to see improved, and with faith it shall be done.

One of the very few areas in which prosperity ministers and I agree is how they critique the often unhelpful way in which Christians discuss suffering. Many Christians say that suffering is necessary; it is essential to being Christlike. I agree that this is not the right approach, but their solution goes too far in the opposite direction: namely, to say that no suffering is necessary for the faithful. I suggest a middle path, one that recognizes that God desires wellbeing for creation but that suffering is an often inevitable result when we are being faithful to the gospel in a world filled with unjust powers. I also agree with them that salvation is something we should be concerned about not just in an afterlife but in our lives now. The *difference* between us is that I see salvation as a collective, societal liberation from what oppresses us, while prosperity gospel adherents think in much more individualistic terms about health and wealth.

Paula White is one of the most famous and highly successful prosperity gospel preachers today. There are several things that she does well: White has a personally compelling story about overcoming abuse and deprivation, has helped thousands of people find hope in the midst of trauma, and she seems genuinely committed to multicultural ministries. All of that is worth affirming. Nevertheless, it cannot absolve her of the abuse inherent in manipulating people through promises of prosperity. She should know better. While advocating for people to donate to her church to receive financial blessings, she is also a major supporter of President Trump (whom I prefer to call "45"). She sees "45" as a vessel for God's work in the world, a modern-day Esther. When White argues that resisting the president's administration is going against the will of God, she is acting in an inherently anti-democratic fashion. In her mind, everything that happens is God's will, whether that is her financial success or the rule of a tyrant. Her solution is to submit to such divinely sanctioned authority. Christians "were sent to take over," she said on the Jim Bakker talk show, not to be servants of all as Jesus taught (Mk. 9:35). As a spiritual guide to the president and as part of his Evangelical Advisory Board, there are currently few religious leaders more influential in terms of having the ear of our highest political officers. Taking a phrase from Christian liturgy, we can say in lament, "Lord have mercy."

Power and Authority Have Been Given to Me

Rather than seeing the Divine as weak, it is better to see the Divine/God as a model for power in our world. Inevitably, the power to dominate, which we erroneously attribute to God, trickles down into the power we give authorities and institutions to dominate for the sake of order. The questions become: Whose order is this? Who benefits? Who is left out? A God of persuasive love and the call to compassion and justice helps us see ourselves in a different light.

How you think about God shapes your understanding of earthly authority. Frequently, authoritarian views of God lead to authoritarian views of human institutions or persons. At the very least, they help justify them. Almost inevitably, those in leadership positions are tempted to cite their authority as a rationale to avoid hard questions. This is especially true of political leadership. The phrases, "Believe me," or, "Only I can save you," are examples of the idolatry of taking up unquestionable authority. Through them, one positions oneself as a messiah, above any questions or reproach. The very act of questioning becomes a traitorous move that undermines the salvation the leader will bring, if only they can go about implementing their program. What does this have to do with God? Authoritarian leaders that mobilize religion *always* frame their work as indicative of divine authorization. Again, take the example of prosperity preachers such as Paula White, who say that "45" has been ordained by God, and that to challenge his agenda is to go against God's will. Talk about an effective way to push people away from religious affiliation!

Of course, some people have argued that God's sovereignty acts as a challenge to human authority. We can see this when radical evil is being committed and faith communities have contrasted God's authority with human authority. Examples include the Barmen Declaration of the Confessing Church against the Third Reich in Germany in the 1930s; the Kairos Document against South African churches supporting apartheid in the 1980s; and the Accra Confession, written in Ghana, against 21st-century neoliberal economic globalization and ecological destruction. All these examples have used the theme of God's authority in contrast with the powers that be. This is an effective theological tool, and I do not want to dismiss it. Our world is better off for having these arguments. Even so, other applications of unquestioning divine authority lead quickly to dangerous places. We see this in debates about sexuality in the Roman Catholic Church today. A reformist Pope like Francis may want to institute changes. He may be sympathetic to officially affirming that unrepentant divorced people can receive communion and confession (it already happens in practice in many places). But to do so he is compelled to avoid saying that previous Popes were in error for coming to the opposite conclusion—for, according to church teaching, Popes can't be wrong on matters of doctrine. How to offer an explicit welcome to divorced persons thus becomes a difficult conundrum to resolve.

Roman Catholics would be far better off with a notion of authority that invites challenge and questioning, as would we all. The biblical story that reflects this dynamic best comes from Mark 7:24–30. In the story, Jesus is traveling far from his home to be alone and away from his regular work. A woman comes to speak with him about her sick daughter. But she is not from his community. She is ethnically other to him. In fact, she is as much an outsider as you can get from his social location. Speaking from his cultural context, Jesus initially dismisses her and her concerns. Rather than being discouraged or unquestioning, she brilliantly turns his dismissal on its head. In effect, she "outsmarts" Jesus. Rather than being indignant, Jesus recognizes her wisdom and says that because of what she has said, her daughter is now well. Yet it doesn't stop there. Soon afterward, Jesus is feeding thousands of people on the Gentile side of the Sea of Galilee, just as he did previously on the Jewish side. Scholars often consider the two feeding miracle stories to be redundant. I suggest instead that they are integral to the evolution of his ministry. The Syrophoenician woman teaches Jesus something new; she helps him extend his ministry beyond its previous limits. That is true divine authority and wisdom—being open enough to change and invite challenge. We should emulate it.

However, not every change brings growth. Some changes are decisive losses. And that challenge leads us to the question of climate change.

What Earth Shall We Inherit?

Jesus said the poor shall inherit the earth (Mt. 5:5). I hope that's true. But we have to ask ourselves what kind of world shall they inherit? Will it be one that is healthy and thriving for all peoples? Or, will it be a wasteland devoid of hope? That latter question may be putting too fine a point on it. Yet, when considering the earth and suffering on it, we have to think about how humans are affecting its future options.

There are perennial social justice issues that affect tens of millions. Not addressing them results in families being torn apart. Traumas are passed generationally through communities. Cycles of crushing poverty, hopelessness, and violence over limited resources persist. In addition to the unnecessary and avoidable pain that these forms of oppression inflict, they are compounded by a complex relationship between each of them with each other. Some actions, and inactions, ripple through the years and centuries. Climate change is one issue our planet is facing that compounds these problems. Unlike some challenges, not addressing this one threatens the very context in which the rest of our struggles can even exist. Not responding to poverty or warfare does not prevent the next generation from acting. This is obviously not an excuse to do nothing, just a question of a qualitative difference in threat. Yet how we respond to issues such as climate change has a more determinative effect, potentially for millennia, unlike anything else in terms of scale besides perhaps nuclear war.

From an emotional perspective, talking about climate change is to be stuck between a rock and a hard place. If you suggest that fixing it involves only minor adjustments to how we organize our economy and society, then you're up against a wall of empirical incredulity. But discussing the real and rising risks and likely results has its own problem: people are overcome by the sheer hopelessness of it all. As a defense mechanism, others dismiss the threats as overblown and hysteria, further delaying meaningful responses.

Let's review what we know through scientific consensus: carbon dioxide and other greenhouse gases are gradually warming our atmosphere. So far the planetary temperature has already increased 1°C (or 1.8°F, for Americans) since the start of the Industrial Age, according to the World Meteorological Organization in 2016.[1] With each degree that global temperatures rise, the risks increase exponentially. There is a broad scientific consensus that an increase of over 2°C from pre-industrial levels puts too much of the planet at an unacceptably high risk. In fact, poorer and low-lying countries argue that anything over 1.5°C is too high of a risk for them. Some might ask, "What's the rush? If it took well over one hundred years to increase the temperature by 1°C; don't we have another hundred years before we have a problem?" Unfortunately, the answer is no.

As climate scientist and friend Jill Craven once helpfully explained to me, emitting greenhouse gases (carbon dioxide and methane, especially) is like setting the temperature on your oven. As anyone who's ever baked something knows, after you set the oven to 400°F, it takes a while for the oven to reach that temperature. Climate change works similarly. The amount of carbon dioxide and other gases we release into the atmosphere now "sets our earth-wide oven" for decades, even centuries to come. Climate scientists have a pretty good idea how much of these greenhouse gases is released from different activities,

---

[1] *World Meteorological Organization Statement on the State of the Global Climate in 2016,* WONo.1189 (Geneva, Switzerland: WMO, 2017), available online at https://library.wmo.int/doc_num.php?explnum_id=3414 .

including burning fossil fuels. They also know roughly how much of these greenhouse gases is necessary for us to reach a planetary temperature increase of 2°C. Bill McKibben, founder of the climate group 350.org, lays out the numbers in grim detail: we only have a two-in-three chance of keeping emissions below 2°C if we release another 800 gigatons worth of carbon dioxide from fossil fuels into the atmosphere. This is a major problem for two reasons: First, human societies worldwide are currently emitting about 40 gigatons per year from fossil fuels.[2] For the math majors out there, that is roughly a path of using up all our climate reserves in 20 years. Obviously, we are not going to reach 2030 and instantly go to the 100 percent abolition of fossil fuels. So, that means that we rapidly have to reduce the amount used, even as the world's population grows and billions of people are climbing out of poverty. Most rich countries grew wealthy in part through rapid industrialization via fossil fuels. However, there were fewer of them then and they had smaller populations too, and so required the use of less fossil fuels. The results are only now becoming fully apparent. Other countries cannot replicate that process without the Earth wildly blowing its "carbon budget." Different forms of development will be necessary, as will financing from wealthy countries to help poor countries with the technological transfers necessary. That's a big lift, and controversial for many, as we will see below.

The second problem is how much of these fossil fuels are actually out there, ready to be burned. Let us just include those fuels (coal, oil, and natural gas) that are currently being extracted from operating facilities, and not including future extraction sites or speculative ventures in impossible to reach places like the Arctic Ocean. Burning them will release approximately 942 gigatons worth of carbon dioxide into the atmosphere, according to a 2016 study released by Oil Change International in partnership with over a dozen climate organizations. If we have 942 gigatons available from current sites,

---

[2] The two relevant articles are: Bill McKibben, "Recalculating the Climate Math," *The New Republic,* posted September 22, 2016, https://newrepublic.com/article/136987/recalculatingclimate-math, and Bill McKibben, "Global Warming's Terrifying New Math," *Rolling Stone,* posted July 19, 2012, https://www.rollingstone.com/politics/news/global-warmings-terrifyingnew-math-20120719.

but only 800 gigatons to use before we exhaust our carbon budget, what does that mean? Essentially, we can't burn all the available resources we have without surpassing the earth's carbon budget. In an earlier 2012 estimate, McKibben was already saying that fully 80 percent of all fossil fuels have to remain unused and in the ground to not exceed our target temperature increase of 2°C. If we are to avoid exceeding the more ecologically just temperature increase of 1.5°C, only 353 out of the 942 currently-available gigatons can be emitted. Economically speaking, this is a problem of obliterating trillions of dollars of wealth—on paper and in investments. Values of fossil fuel companies, including people's pensions, are based on the assumption that the resources a fossil fuel company has will actually be used. If 80 percent or more of their paper wealth is removed, that means huge financial losses for some very powerful people and companies. We should expect those companies and heavily invested individuals will fight tooth and nail to delay or obscure this reality. By keeping alive the illusion of a scientific debate on the reality of climate change, they can delay laws and regulations that would force such changes to their bottom line. In fact, they *are already* doing this quite actively.

A fair question to ask at this point is "What's the big deal about 2°C of warming, anyway?" It would be one thing if this merely meant a slightly warmer winter for everyone. After all, who would really mind an average winter high in Kentucky increasing from 42°F to 45.5°F? Unfortunately, this perspective assumes that everything else stays the same except for the temperature. As climate activist Bill McKibben has quipped, it's not so much global warming as "global weirding" that we should be worried about. Permanent climate changes affect far more than temperature. When weather patterns change, places at risk of seasonal droughts and wildfires receive even *more irregular* rain, while wet areas receive more flooding. Big shifts in temperature in places of high humidity increase the risk of tornados, extending that deadly season.

More critically, weather patterns in the extreme north and south of the planet experience greater temperature increases than does the rest of the planet. So, the planet may warm 2°C overall, but some areas warm 5° to 6°C, while other regions' temperatures may remain flat or even decrease slightly. The poles hold the vast majority of glaciers, which are melting and threatening disruptive sea level rise. Increasingly melting permafrost in Canada and Russia risks the release of even more, previously frozen, methane gas into the atmosphere (more greenhouse gas!). Even if we can get our fossil fuel use under control at some point, we risk passing certain tipping points, in which feedback loops accelerate climate change, and the release of additional greenhouse gases increases—even if humans halt their own greenhouse gas contributions.

Not surprisingly, these changes already affect the world's communities unevenly. As annoying as it is to have a drought last longer in southern California, it hasn't yet personally affected me much. Even as I write this sentence in December 2017, over 200,000 people in California have fled wildfires. Yet even fires within one hundred miles of my apartment did not change my schedule or activities; for others, it has been life-altering. It seems that unless a crisis is crashing through their windows, most people ignore it. Zombie films make this a central insight about human nature: we go about our daily lives until the crisis is at our doorstep. Countless others around the world can no longer ignore what is happening. Some Pacific island countries, such as the Solomon Islands, are already disappearing beneath rising sea levels (the Solomons have lost at least five islands so far), and others will soon follow, forcing their inhabitants to relocate. Droughts from climate change have exacerbated rural displacement in Syria, increasing tensions in urban areas before its civil war began in 2011. Climate refugees are an increasingly common occurrence, including thousands leaving Puerto Rico after climate change strengthened an already devastating hurricane in 2017. There are people living in my community who are homeless and face an increased risk of heat exhaustion by being outside in the summertime. While some of us see this as a mere theoretical threat to future generations, whole portions of the planet have formed a consensus that climate change is hurting them now, and even *yesterday*.

Even during the Obama administration, the political responses from the U.S. in particular were half-hearted and far too minimal. Sure, they were steps in the right direction. Yes, increase gas mileage requirements on new cars. Yes, add regulations forcing refineries to reduce emissions. Yes, transition away from coal and sign the Paris Climate Accord. But even at their boldest, they were only bold from the stance of political possibility, not empirical necessity. Cutting fossil fuel emissions in the U.S. by 25 percent from 2005 levels is good, but what is actually needed is a path toward fossil fuel abolition by 2030. The best you could say is they were steps in the right direction, which we could build upon.

Yet, *now,* our country is making a U-turn back toward the past like there's no tomorrow. It's true that hundreds of cities and many state governments are resisting such backward motion. But this is an all-hands-on-deck moment. If you pull on the emergency brake to stop a speeding train from going over a ravine, that won't help much if, at the same time, someone is shoveling more coal to fuel the engine. Though as a country we may be able to meet our emission reduction commitments, even after "45" withdrew us from the Paris Climate Accord (thanks to rapidly growing solar and wind power), the U.S. won't be standing by its promise to fund the transition for poorer countries. This was the part of the Accord that "45" thought was unjust. The idea that different countries, with different histories of emissions, wealth, and historical culpability would have different responsibilities to each other was not something that even crossed his mind. Yes, China pollutes more than the U.S. overall per year, but, *historically,* the U.S. is the #1 emitter. On a per person basis, we continue to emit far more than either China or India. So, yes, we have a special responsibility to help other countries to not follow our path, and to help them transition to clean energy as fast as possible. You could even say we owe an *ecological debt* to other countries for having burned more than our fair share of fossil fuels, and vastly more than the planet can safely absorb.

At the very time it is most critical for the planet's societies to work together, such pleas are falling on deaf ears. It would be too much to say that climate activists are trying to save the world. What we are trying to save is civilization as we know it. No, better yet, we are trying to transform ourselves into a civilization that is sustainable for the long haul and worth saving by being more just. We know that there have already been five mass extinctions in the 4.5 billion year history of our planet, periods in which at least half of all the species went extinct in a relatively short period. Some scientists say we are entering the sixth mass extinction. In two million years, the planet will be fine. However, that is cold comfort to every human who exists or will exist.

Likewise, indigenous communities remind us that this would not be the first time that "the world ended." Previous iterations of the end of the world as people knew it were in the late 15th and early 16th centuries in the areas of Mexico, the Caribbean, and South America. Whole civilizations were wiped out, with the scattered survivors left to pick up the pieces. But this time, it is we who are feeling the threat. It's our turn, and many of us either despair or turn our faces from the coming cataclysm—pretending it doesn't exist, and, in so doing, making it more likely to come to pass.

Some activists feel that we've already waited too long to halt the worst effects of climate change. The types of societal changes that are necessary are so gargantuan that they have become politically impossible. Since those with the most power to change our practices are the same people who feel the effects of climate change less and later than others, it's too late. Zhiwa Woodbury is probably the most well-known person in what is called the "planetary hospice movement." His big claim is that, as with a person who has to learn how to grieve before a loved one dies, we have to learn how to grieve for a planet on which life as we know it will die. That doesn't mean that we should give up or stop caring. It is not an excuse to do as we please. How a person dies, in comfort, with loved ones supporting them, is valuable in and of itself. If someone has a parent with a terminal illness and they never visit them because they think, "What's the point? They are going to die soon anyway," we would agree that this person is missing something important. Similarly, those who advocate for planetary hospice argue that life as we know it will be as good as dead. We should take time to grieve, continue to care for the earth, and honor the coming deaths as we approach the sixth great mass extinction, this one caused by the decisions and indecisions of collective human failings.

Perhaps less bleak is the perspective of the theologian John Cobb, who already—*over 40 years ago*—was writing about an ecological crisis and asking whether it was too late to prevent it. Concluding that it is indeed too late to save life as we know it, he recommends focusing on building communities that will survive in a less hospitable future after a larger collapse of civilization. Just as after the Roman Empire fell there were many Christian monastic communities that went into "the desert" to find new life together, so Cobb suggests a similar approach for today. Whether or not you agree with the level of crisis that Cobb says we are facing, I certainly appreciate the commitment to forming communities of resilience and strengthening those that already exist. If society does collapse, these communities will be necessary tools to preserve some of the human values we cherish. And if things turn around, they can be seen as leading examples that pull the broader society toward a better future. Either way, to do something proactive seems like a win-win. Win or lose, we are charged with holding fast to the vision of a healthy world for all. It's less about "believing" in that as an idea, and more about actively living like it is already true, come what may.

Faithfulness to God's Vision

Sometimes the way we translate passages in the Bible obscures important insights. This is particular true when we think about "faith." We think faith is about belief rather than lived embodiment, grounded in our deepest convictions. Probably one of the worst offenders is Romans 3:22. The assumption that we are saved by grace through faith, influenced by the early Protestant interpretation of Christianity, means that there is an incentive to skew this passage. The NRSV (New Revised Standard Version)

> *Our faithfulness to God's vision is worth it, even if the world dismisses us as losers.*

translation reads: "the righteousness of God through faith in Jesus Christ for all who believe." But there is a little footnote that offers a different translation. Instead of "faith in Jesus Christ," in reads "through the faith of Jesus Christ." Well, which is it? Having faith in Jesus, or having the faith of Jesus? The former is about assent to an idea, of trusting him. But just as easily and, frankly, more compellingly, Paul could be understood to mean that righteousness comes not from our belief in Jesus, but the belief of Jesus. Faith is not so much about believing in him, but taking up his mantle and doing likewise. Righteousness comes through Jesus's faithfulness to God's vision, and we participate in that righteousness when we become Christ's body on earth and go and do likewise. Jesus calls us to represent and reflect God's vision for our world, a vision for which Jesus so earnestly lived and died that his way remains just as powerful nearly 2000 years after the fact.

Our faithfulness to God's vision is worth it, even if the world dismisses us as losers. In spite of the setbacks, losses, and likely heartache at not seeing the fruits of our labor, we are not alone, and our efforts are not in vain. Witnessing to the good news of a world healed and full of justice is valuable in its own right, even if people do not respond to this message. We may be ridiculed, we may be persecuted, we may even end up walking the way of the cross if we get organized and the powers-that-be see us as a threat. But our faithfulness—win, lose, or draw—is worth it.

Theological Leanings Quiz

INSTRUCTIONS: Answer each question by selecting one of five choices—A, B, C, D, or E—that most closely reflects your perspective.

1. What is the core problem of life?
   A. Unrealized potential
   B. Personal sin
   C. Personal misfortune
   D. Ignorance
   E. Bondage of others

2. Who or what is God/the Divine?
   A. It's irrelevant: people may have found God meaningful in the past, but less so today
   B. Revelation: known through the death and resurrection of Jesus Christ
   C. A responder who provides blessing and security to those who ask
   D. An inclusive being who loves everyone just as they are

E. A table-turner who demands an end to oppressive systems

3. Why do bad things happen to good people?
    A. Because of bad luck
    B. Because of the free will of humans
    C. Because they don't demand a blessing
    D. I'm not sure, but I trust we are loved
    E. Because of unjust forces or powers that hurt others

4. What does salvation look like?
    A. I'm not interested in that
    B. Heaven after I die and a personal relationship with Jesus now
    C. Personal health and wealth
    D. The term "salvation" makes me vaguely uneasy
    E. Healthy communities free from violence and injustice

5. What is the role of religious congregations?
    A. To live and let live; just don't make me go!
    B. To motivate us to overcome temptation
    C. To empower us to name and claim what is ours
    D. To offer fellowship and service
    E. To witness to the coming kingdom of God on earth

6. To what extent are religions besides Christianity true?
    A. They are all equally wrong, including Christianity
    B. Their religion does not save them, but the people can be nice
    C. They need to call on the right name for help
    D. They are all equally true; we all need to get along and see our similarities
    E. They are true to the degree that they are working for a just world

7. Which of these is most important to you in this life?
    A. Self-realization
    B. Saving souls
    C. Prosperity for family

D. Respect of difference

E. Strength in the face of adversity

8. What's the proper place of religion in politics?

    A. It's unconstitutional; religions should stay out of politics

    B. To ensure a moral and biblical order

    C. To lift up political leaders whom God has chosen

    D. Religion is already too political

    E. To work for social transformation

*Your results: Add up how many of each letter you chose as answers. The letter that you chose the most indicates your theological lens. It is possible to lean in more than one direction. Go to page **113** to see what your leanings are.*

CHAPTER 3 DISCUSSION QUESTIONS

• Is a God who cannot stop evil from happening but is with us in the struggle worth following? Why or why not?

• How do you respond to the claim that the prosperity gospel is an anti-gospel? Are there any televangelists that you admire or believe share a gospel of actual good news? What do they do differently than other TV personalities?

• In the face of such great threats to our planet, what do you do to persevere and not give up?

• Is hospice an ethical metaphor for responding to the threat of climate change? What might that look like?

• How do you react to the notion that we can be faithful and yet lose?

For Further Reading

Cobb, John B. Jr. *Is It Too Late? A Theology of Ecology*. 1972. Reprint. Denton, Texas: Environmental Ethics Books, 1995.

_____. *The Process Perspective: Frequently Asked Questions about Process Theology*. Edited by Jeanyne B. Slettom. St. Louis: Chalice Press, 2003.

Epperly, Bruce G. *Process Theology: A Guide for the Perplexed*. New York: T&T Clark International, 2011.

Keller, Catherine. *On the Mystery: Discerning Divinity in Process*. Minneapolis: Fortress Press, 2008.

Klein, Naomi. *This Changes Everything: Capitalism vs. the Climate*. New York: Simon & Schuster, 2014.

Lull, David, and John B. Cobb Jr. *Romans (Chalice Commentaries for Today)*. St. Louis: Chalice Press, 2005.

Marshall, George. *Don't Even Think about It: Why Our Brains Are Wired to Ignore Climate Change*. New York: Bloomsbury U.S., 2015.

Mesle, C. Robert. *Process Theology: A Basic Introduction*. St. Louis: Chalice Press, 1993.

Pope Francis. *Laudato Si': On Care for Our Common Home*. Encyclical Letter. Vatican City: Libreria Editrice Vaticana, 2015.

4

Perseverance amidst Injustice

For over a generation, the mascot of the battery company Duracell has been the Energizer Bunny. Pink, with sunglasses and a bass drum, it never stops moving. As Duracell's tagline says, he keeps going and going. I admit I don't know about the actual quality of Duracell batteries as opposed to other options. (I use rechargeable ones myself.) Even so, it is an apt image for the need to persevere. You have to keep going and going. This is especially true when we are hit by setbacks. This chapter is about perseverance amidst injustice. How did those weighed down by oppression long ago and those who persevere today endure in the struggle for a better world, despite obstacles? Those who struggle for justice without giving up help us see the world and its needed transformation from the underside of history. It is about looking with the eyes of the victims of evil, those who are pressed down in the game of domination. Their perseverance can teach all of us a great deal.

Being Ahistorical

Like most Americans, progressives frequently have a weak appreciation for history. The latest outrage coming from the President, white nationalists, or white domestic terrorists provokes an outcry that "this is not our country." Normatively, they are correct. Such exclusive and alienating values are antithetical to what America has been at its best. But *descriptively,* their comments are ahistorical to the point of naïveté. An example of this tendency was used to great comedic effect on the first Saturday Night Live episode directly following the 2016 U.S. presidential election. In a skit, a group of white progressives plans to celebrate Hillary Clinton's presumed victory. As the night wears on, its members become increasingly anxious as election results come in. They go from being optimistic, to rationalizing, to sullen, and finally despondent. Eventually, two black friends, Chris Rock and Dave Chappelle, join the party-turned-mortuary. The white attendees exclaim at the news of the presidential results, "This is the worst thing America has ever done!" Rock and Chappelle look at each other, pause for a beat, and start laughing out loud.

It is hard to be shocked when you have a firm foundation in the history of America's racial legacy. Actions may disappoint you, but they will not shock you. From the terrorism of white extremists to the seemingly mundane rules of police use-of-force practices, our policies cast a pall on any naïve narratives of innocence. It is this contrast between narratives of innocence and the experience of dehumanization that organizations such as Black Lives Matter unmask. This unveiling of who we are is likely the reason why so many whites vehemently resist this framing. This is true even for those who self-identify as progressive. A different story can threaten our sense of self. To accept other communities' experiences of our country as valid is to become critical of stories of American innocence and progress as the only ones we can tell. Taking this step can be a traumatic experience psychically. It is not equivalent to the trauma of being targeted by police, obviously, yet it demands that one reorient how one understands oneself in the world.

While it is a common observation in activist circles, it bears repeating: the United States was founded on violence and exploitation. Nearly four hundred years ago, African slaves were brought to work on plantations for their white masters. Colonization of the "New World" also meant the appropriation of indigenous land and genocidal practices to remove the indigenous peoples from the land. Slavery's 250-year history and the legacy of violence against indigenous people are central to the American experience. Slaves built the White House. In the 19th century, immigrants were brought to work on railroads, plantations, and other industries, and endured rampant exploitation and cultural discrimination. The histories that most American children still read focus on heroic, mythical individuals who demonstrated the pioneering spirit. Only in recent decades has a wider audience heard the voices of victims of that very spirit. An excellent example of this is the now-classic book, *A People's History of the United States* by Howard Zinn, which retells American history from the accounts and perspectives of those on its underside.

Amidst centuries of abuse and violence, different groups have found ways to survive. Many of the early African American spirituals are about a promise of a better future in heaven, when no justice can be found on earth. Others explicitly address the great cloud of witnesses and ancestors who went before and persevered in spite of it all. Perhaps the most influential example in this style is the hymn, "Lift Every Voice and Sing," sometimes referred to as the Black National Anthem. Verse two expresses this sentiment most explicitly:

> *Stony the road we trod, Bitter the chast'ning rod,*
> *Felt in the days when hope unborn had died;*
> *Yet with a steady beat, Have not our weary feet*
> *Come to the place for which our people sighed?*
> *We have come over a way that with tears has been watered*
> *We have come, treading our path through the blood of the slaughtered;*
> *Out from the gloomy past, Till now we stand at last*
> *Where the bright gleam of our bright star is cast.*

I didn't understand what was being articulated when I first heard this sung. I didn't know its cultural context, and some of the language bothered me greatly. The phrase "treading our path through the blood of the slaughtered" sounded to my ears like a holy war proclamation of destroying our enemies in the name of God. I didn't realize immediately that it was actually the *singers' ancestors* who were the victims being killed. The hymn reveals a profound sense of connection between "what has come before" and "where we are now." It expresses the insight that, in spite of the struggle people have endured, they have arrived at a better place. It doesn't soft-pedal past trauma; it goes through it to the other side. That appreciation for the great cloud of witnesses, those who struggled to survive and find meaning and hope in dire situations, is something that many Americans need to relearn. Or learn for the first time.

If hymns aren't your thing, a slightly more recent song speaks to the American historical struggle and our ongoing response to it: Billy Joel's "We Didn't Start the Fire." The chorus begins as follows:

We didn't start the fire
It was always burning since the world's been turning

Highlighting a variety of American experiences—some cultural, some silly, some international—Joel implies that we are part of a long chain of struggle, one that we can expect to go on indefinitely into the future. Even if we didn't cause the problems we currently face, we are charged with responding to the best of our ability. We must address them faithfully, even if the fire morphs and continues burning long after we are gone.

Naïveté in the Face of Evil

I was raised to respect people, to help others, and to welcome people and perspectives different from my own experience. In this way I was fortunate, but my upbringing also left me with a blind spot: an instinctive resistance to assume the worst in people's intentions. It's hard to accept the idea that people are willfully screwing people over. In general, I tend to want to separate notions of intent from discussions of impact. Yes, the impact of an action or decision is systemically hurting others, and certain groups are the primary culprits. But whether they are knowingly or willfully hurting people is something I want to sidestep.

Part of this instinct is practical. It is very difficult to prove other persons' intentions. All they have to do is deny them or say that you cannot see into another person's heart. Unless you have an audio clip of them explicitly disclosing their true motives, proof is elusive. It seems preferable to focus on the demonstrable effects of their actions. These are far easier to prove and respond to. This is a standard technique in anti-racism trainings when talking to white people about racism and their "good intentions." People want to focus on their intentions and what is in their hearts, and they need help to see that intent matters less than impact. As civil rights activists like the Rev. James Lawson have said for decades, the problem of plantation slavery wasn't that white people didn't like black people; the problem was they systemically exploited them.

In spite of this, it is problematic to refuse to see willful intent to commit evil. It's far outside many of our usual everyday experiences— but for other people, it is something they see every day of their lives. Like most people raised in liberal households, progressives often have the bias that education will solve most problems. The idea that people will learn and yet persist in hurting others falls outside that scheme. It can sound conspiratorial to us. However, it is less difficult to imagine if we look at some examples of the past evil intent of certain institutions. If these things happened in the past, and if humans as a group tend to not change, that makes it reasonable to assume that there are people actively doing likewise in our day and age. I offer two examples: the British Empire pushing opium in 19th-century China, and the oil company Exxon deliberately delaying public knowledge of the climate science consensus.

Let us start with British trade with China. The British Empire developed a three-way trade route with India and China in the 17th to 19th centuries. Silver, opium, and tea were the main trading items. Tea came from China, silver from Britain, and opium from India. Before long, tea became so important to British culture that almost 10 percent of its GDP went to purchasing it. China, on the other hand, was primarily a self-contained economy. It didn't need anything made in Britain, and its officials considered most of what the British brought them toys and purely optional items. They were happy to take Britain's silver but were not purchasing much in return. However, Britain wanted its money back. It essentially had a massive trade deficit. It gave silver to China and purchased tea, but it wasn't selling much of anything to recoup its tea imports.

Over several decades, British officials noticed that their ships were selling increasing amounts of opium on their trade trips to China. They decided that increasing opium sales would be a way to recoup some of the money they had spent on tea. So, they intentionally ramped up the opium supply in China. With the exponential growth in sales, by the early 19th century opium use had reached the point where it was becoming a social problem in China. When China resisted the import of opium and demanded that its sale cease, Britain defeated Chinese coastal military forces and gained major trade concessions. This led to ports being opened and the eventual creation of the major trade city of Hong Kong, which was held by Britain until 1997. Intentionally flooding a country with socially destabilizing drugs to increase your trade balance sounds horrendous. How could people do such a thing? Yet British officials did this, and they did it with intent. If it happened then and there, is it so far-fetched to consider analogous evil acts happening here and now?

In the 20th century, the oil company ExxonMobil's own scientists determined that fossil fuels were contributing to climate change.[1] The company began making investments in Arctic regions on the assumption that climate change was happening and that polar ice would increasingly be absent during the summertime in the Northern Hemisphere. By buying drilling rights early, they would have access to these future drilling sites at a lower cost than if they waited for the melting to occur. It was a smart business move in terms of narrow self-interest and future profitability. But even as the investment branch of Exxon was acting upon the research their own scientists were telling them, the public relations branch was working overtime to muddy the waters on the public perception of the reality of climate change.

Exxon realized that they didn't need to convince people that climate change wasn't happening. All they needed to do was create a

---

[1] Articles from the 2015 investigative series can be found here: "Exxon: The Road Not Taken," *Inside Climate News,* posts from Sept. 16-Dec. 22, 2015, https://insideclimatenews.org/content/Exxon-The-Road-Not-Taken. For an academic study confirming these reports, see: Geoffrey Supran and Naomi Oreskes, "Assessing ExxonMobil's climate change communications (1977-2014)," *Environmental Research* Volume 12:8. IOP Publishing, August 23, 2017.

two-sided controversy, in which the average person listening in on the radio or TV could reasonably say: "There's an active debate." This is particularly true when most media interviews on controversial topics have two guest speakers. This makes for easy false equivalencies. One objective, in which Exxon was largely successful, was to delay any social consensus on the reality of climate change. Their primary goal was to delay any positive actions that would inhibit additional fossil fuel extraction projects. To that end, they hired attorneys like Ted Wells, who the cigarette giant Philip Morris had used previously to obfuscate the truth and then delay a consensus on the dangers of smoking.

From an amoral business perspective, what Exxon did was brilliant. By delaying a social and political consensus, they have been able to continue to profit from the extraction of fossil fuels decades after the pertinent facts were in. While they haven't been able to drill in the Arctic yet, they have maintained substantial profits. Of course, while businesses may bracket issues of ethics and morality from their decisions, millions of people are impacted and placed in significant peril. Put bluntly, Exxon made money knowing that their actions would endanger life on the planet and its communities for generations, if not centuries. This involved not just impact but intentions. That is evil.

I'm sure Exxon's decision makers found rationales for their actions to help them sleep at night. They had a duty to their shareholders. Technology would resolve climate change through innovation, they may have thought. Scientific models are predictions and subject to revision, they rationalized. I'm sure there were other mental gymnastics. At the end of the day, such self-justifications remind

> *Liberal-minded people often confuse education with the solution.*

us that evil is present in our world. It doesn't have to look like Dr. Evil of the Austin Powers' films, maniacally rubbing its hands together as it holds the world hostage from certain doom. In fact, evil usually appears quite banal. Just doing one's job, trying to get ahead, and dismissing the consequences for those one does not value is the shape of systemic evil today. It's actually not hard to be evil; all that is necessary is to feel nothing concerning the consequences one's decisions will have for others. What is needed is to distance oneself from their voices, faces, and bodies—both physically and emotionally. Once one does that, almost anything is possible—whether collateral civilian damage from engaging in warfare, condemning poor people to concentrated poverty with few opportunities for improvement, or undermining the human habitability of the planet.

Education or raising awareness is an insufficient response to such problems. In the Exodus story in the Bible, Egypt's Pharaoh knew of the cries of the Hebrews. He saw what he was doing to them. He didn't need Moses to tell him what was happening. *He knew.* But he didn't care; he felt nothing; his heart was hardened (Ex. 8:32). Liberal-minded people often confuse education with the solution. They are correct that people need to know what is happening in matters of injustice, but knowledge alone will not create needed changes. It may be necessary, but it is not sufficient to move enough people to act, resist, and offer alternatives. Two people can roughly agree on the facts but disagree that something should be done; if one of them feels nothing in response to another's suffering, no amount of information will change that. What is required is a conversion of the heart, a transformation in how people see themselves and others. That cannot be forced. As the old saying goes, you can lead a horse to water, but you can't make it drink. You can give someone all the information in the world, but you can't make them feel empathy, remorse, or compassion. Certain experiences can help make such changes more likely, but there is no guarantee. At the end of the day, Pharaoh can still choose to harden his heart, as can we all. One of the ways we see such hardened hearts is around escalating hatred against immigrants in our country.

When We Are the Last Legitimate Immigrants

I was born in the United States, as were my parents, grandparents, and great-grandparents. But if I go back a few more generations, I find that I am the descendant of immigrants. One great-great-grandfather came from Ireland alone as a child; my middle name honors his first name: Charles. If I look further back across other lines of descent, I find ancestors from England, Germany, the Netherlands, Scandinavia, and France. None of them had proper papers. They boarded ships, left everything they knew, and made homes for themselves in the United States. But if they did the exact same thing today, they would be considered undocumented, or, pejoratively, "illegal." It wasn't until the early 20th century that regulations about "proper documents" went into effect, in part as a xenophobic backlash against newer waves of less-Protestant immigrants. Lamentably, many people whose ancestors benefited from the relatively lax legal requirements are quick to pull up the ladders they had previously climbed that allowed them authorized entry and opportunities.

It has been over 30 years since the last great amnesty of 1986. Many people had entered the United States without recognition, often as refugees from civil conflicts in Central America that the U.S. exacerbated. Eventually, it became necessary that they be given the status they were due. But the pressure has been building for decades now. For those with historical memory, 2006 won't seem that long ago. For others with the luxury to ignore it, it's ancient history. But 2006 was when the first great contemporary effort to reform immigration policies in the U.S. was attempted. Under consideration was a mishmash of legal recognition, benefits to major corporations, reunification of families, and penalties for not following the proper channels. Though it was a compromise that many found distasteful, especially because of its corporate leanings, it appeared to be the best option then available to expand human rights in the United States. But it failed. In spite of over a half a million people in the spring of 2006 mobilizing in the streets for a day without immigrants, by that summer no legal changes were forthcoming. Nationwide rallies had stopped terrible new policies from being enacted, like making it illegal to offer social services or food to undocumented people. In that regard, those rallies were a victory against disaster, but they were unable to ensure nationwide positive changes.

In the ensuing years, undocumented immigrants have been somewhat stuck. For every state that expands in-state tuition to college-bound undocumented students who grew up here, another state prohibits it. For every state that allows undocumented persons to earn drivers' licenses, there are more that set up checkpoints in immigrant neighborhoods and conduct sweeps that terrorize communities. For over ten years, we have been at a relative impasse. Those who say that immigration is one of their top priorities are relatively few, and many of them actually want *further* restrictions on both undocumented and even *legal* immigration. During this time, we've seen the New Sanctuary Movement, the fight for Dreamers, the *new* New Sanctuary Movement, and years of organizing among local faith groups and immigrant communities to demand undocumented immigrants be treated with respect and dignity, including ending the separation of parents and children seeking asylum. The fight isn't over. There is no guarantee that things will get better and not become worse. The current U.S. administration's perspective on immigrants makes it all but certain that there will be no easy progress. Previous mobilizing efforts in 2009, 2010, and 2013 argued that "*this* time" we can win once and for all. But those with the long vision saw that regardless of *this* legislative cycle or *that* proposed bill, the larger work is for the long haul. Pinning all one's hopes on a single moment risks the loss of faith once that idol is smashed.

At the same time, certain idols need to be smashed. They separate us from the sufferings of others. They keep us from learning from the perseverance of persecuted and exploited communities. One such idol that needs dethroning is the ideology of "whiteness."

Against Whiteness

The most damaging part of being white in America is the lack of a sense of one's history. By "white," I don't mean having fair skin. Most white people, naïve of their whiteness, seem to think that people who criticize them are criticizing their external features. While some rhetoric leans in that direction (the classic "blue-eyed devil" trope, for instance), the strongest critiques of whiteness are ideological. Being white has nothing to do with having blue/green eyes or blonde/red hair. People for thousands of years had such features but were not *ideologically* white. That's why the statement, "There is nothing good about being white," is so accurate ideologically and so confusing from a superficial, external understanding. Becoming white involves the unlearning of one's ancestral heritage—whether Germanic, Irish,

Norwegian, or some other ethnic heritage. That heritage is erased and replaced with a system in which white supremacy dominates other racial groups. Ideologically, whiteness only exists as something with which to dominate "non-white" peoples. It has no intrinsic value on its own, only the value it extracts from other groups who cannot fit within its shifting mold.

One obvious complication is that most white Americans do not have a single ethnic heritage and tradition they can reclaim directly. There are certainly some whose parents or grandparents immigrated to the United States. For them, it is easier to make a fairly direct line back to some specific country of origin. But those whose ancestors have been here for a century or more are usually hybrids across multiple traditions. The whole point of American policies of European immigration was to create a new people freed from Europe's influences. The cost was creating whiteness as a new identity. It was an endeavor that was largely successful. Just as the problem is one that was made across generations, its solution will take generations. This effort can only be sustained by communities that are dedicated to this transformation over the long haul. Through such transformation, they can begin to appreciate the wisdom of their sisters and brothers. When white people break free of the ideology of white supremacy, they can hear insights for their own healing. One set of voices they need to listen to on contemporary perseverance comes from Black Lives Matter.

Learning from Black Lives Matter

Since 2014, Black Lives Matter has taken on national significance—first in Ferguson, Missouri, and eventually in forming chapters across the country and even internationally. Woefully or willfully misunderstood by its detractors as a "reverse racism" organization, its name has always implied "too" at the end of its name. As in: "Black lives matter, *too*," not: "Black lives matter *only*." What I admire so much about the Black Lives Matter movement is not just the willingness of countless people to organize. People have risked state reprisals by engaging in nonviolent direct actions, such as blocking highways or entrances to city buildings to demand that their grievances be heard. In fact, most Americans only know about the rallies and marches as outcries. But a second and perhaps even more important long-term component of the movement is not so much the notion of resistance but that of resilience.

Black Lives Matters events are also about forming a sense of dignity and power. These provide meaning making for those who see that their lives do not matter to our dominant systems. They are a way of saying, "We are still here. We are not going anywhere." Unless you witness these actions, you often miss this dynamic, which is never addressed in major news outlets. After the outcry at the latest extrajudicial killing or assault by police officers, often including testimonies from family members, there is a shift. Beyond the specific details of the local problems, there is a second component: a broader affirmation of Blackness. This includes open-mike sharing of testimonies from the community, prayers (often from Afrocentric traditions such as Ifa), singing, and music. These elements focus less on the negative atrocity and more on the power of living and being seen as valuable in each other's eyes.

When four hundred years of precedent demonstrate the intransigence of white supremacy and institutional oppression, it strains credibility to declare that all will be made right in a moment. At its best, Black Lives Matter reflects this recognition that the oppression Black people experience has long historical antecedents. So do Black efforts at resiliency. Black Lives Matter witnesses to being part of this long chain of struggle across generations and ancestors, and offers hope that an alternative is possible. It exemplifies the previous insight that we must demand everything *now* in order to obtain some of it *eventually*. While the policies may struggle to shift, building a broader pro-black culture within oppressed persons is a goal that can be realized on the journey.

Standing Rock Stands Together

This perseverance of communities coming together was wonderfully expressed in the 2016 efforts of the Standing Rock Lakota Nation to halt the Dakota Access Pipeline. That April, a number of Standing

Rock members, along with allies from nearby indigenous nations, set up the Sacred Stone Camp outside of Cannon Ball, North Dakota. Their purpose was to pray for the rivers and oppose the planned Dakota Access Pipeline through what is traditional indigenous land. Over the course of several months, international attention gathered around this effort and other nearby sites, where "water protectors" committed to staying until the federal government canceled the proposed pipeline. Along with nonviolent direct action, lawsuits were brought against the federal government, arguing that indigenous tribal members had not been adequately consulted prior to construction.

State and private security forces, including the North Dakota National Guard, mercilessly cracked down on supporters and those staying at the camps. Protesters experienced attacks from dogs, tear gas, and water cannons in sub-freezing temperatures. Internal government documents referred to the activists as akin to proto-terrorists and a threat to national security. In the late fall of 2016, a shift occurred. In light of the violence being committed against the water protectors, several thousand former U.S. veterans, many of them of indigenous heritage, committed to go to Standing Rock. They would act as a barrier to protect those who were trying to prevent the pipeline's completion. With mounting pressure, the Army Corps of Engineers halted the pipeline section through indigenous land in December of 2016, requiring a full environmental impact report. Celebrations broke out in North Dakota and around the country. Finally, here was a victory to show what was possible when people come together on behalf of their rights and the rights of the earth! With this victory and winter with its sub-zero temperatures entering the camp, elders of the Standing Rock reservation encouraged the camp to disband.

Within two weeks of the Trump administration taking office, however, the new president signed a memorandum expediting the construction of the pipeline, with the pipeline resuming construction in early February 2017. However, by June 2017 a U.S. District Court determined that the Army Corps of Engineers had violated the law by not doing a full environmental impact report and acknowledged the previously ignored right of affected communities to be consulted. In

October 2017, a federal judge ruled that the pipeline could remain open during the environmental review process, which was appealed by Standing Rock in June 2018. As of this writing, it is unknown what the final result will be of the pipeline and its effects on the Missouri River and communities that depend on it for a water source. Even so, the organizational efforts around preventing it model the struggle for a better world in spite of intense oppression.

While most of the media attention was focused on the indigenous community there, the campaign consisted of a much broader movement. Rather than being a single indigenous nation rising up to resist the pipeline and its ecological and cultural threat, it was much more. We witnessed the largest intertribal gathering of support and solidarity since General George Custer's defeat at the Battle of Little Bighorn, over 140 years ago. While the immediate purpose of the activism was to protect the Missouri River from the Dakota Access Pipeline, there was a second feature that may have an even greater long-term impact. This multinational indigenous convening was just as much about indigenous organizing, for it highlighted the daily actions and rituals that undergirded the work of the water protectors. Consequently, this campaign and the relationship-building it launched has had ripple effects in other areas. With the encampment dispersed as winter set in and the seeming victory over the Obama administration to temporarily halt construction, various tribal organizers returned to their particular settings, promising to fight fossil fuel infrastructure projects in their own backyards. While less prevalent in our current media climate, such efforts persist and inspire on local and regional levels.

What lessons does Standing Rock provide to those of us who care deeply about justice and about the communities directly impacted by an existing or proposed action having a say in what happens in their environment? There are several things we can be confident about: those who seek to profit at the expense of the earth and oppressed people will always look for a loophole to continue doing what they want to do. So long as there is financial profit to be made, someone will try to exploit it. They will hire attorneys; they will meet with politicians; they will have the implicit/explicit support of state authorities with the use of force on their side. None of this should be surprising or considered out of the ordinary.

What does the Standing Rock Lakota Nation have? They can file legal petitions, forcibly block construction, and ask for support from allies across the spectrum. But what makes all of this sustainable is the power of community. Whether they win or have a setback, it is the ability to gather and not feel isolated or powerless that helps movements for justice and healing persist over the long term. Anyone can go to an action or one-off vigil. People can romanticize "fighting the power." But to endure over the long term, actions need communities. Communities oriented to a spatial location can be powerful forces of perseverance when organized. As we will see in the next vignette, they can also attract violent opposition.

Crucified for a Dam

The Lenca are the largest indigenous group in Honduras. They have endured for thousands of years as empires, kingdoms, conquerors, and invaders have risen up around them. In spite of it all, they have persisted. Most of their settlements are located along major rivers, which has put them in conflict with various forces of transnational capitalism today. Maintaining access to these historic areas is crucially connected to their human rights. Often, multinational companies and even their own government use the rhetoric of development and progress to justify the Lenca's displacement and ignore their human rights. Amidst the onslaught of outside forces, there have been victories amidst losses. The proposed construction of a hydroelectric dam threatened those Lenca who lived along the Rio Blanco. The dam would have displaced their entire community. Its construction had been attempted without the community's input or informed consent. This effort came after the 2009 U.S.-backed coup against Honduras's democratically elected government, an action repeatedly defended by Hillary Clinton during the 2016 Democratic primary. After organizing within their community and mobilizing peaceful marches through the capital and through makeshift roadblocks, the Lenca successfully stopped the Agua Zarca Dam from being built. This 2014 victory had a ripple effect that angered transnational companies, including those that would have profited from the mining facility the dam was intended to power.[2]

In the struggle to halt the dam, many people were injured or killed by government-backed and U.S.-supported military and company forces. Sustained by their spirituality and connection to place, a number of the Lenca have walked the way of the cross. One of their leaders, Berta Cáceres, received the 2015 Goldman Environmental Prize for her courageous organizing in the face of multinational opposition. (Readers can watch an inspiring and informative YouTube video that the Goldman Environmental Prize produced at that time.) For many, Cáceres became the international face of their struggle and the voice demanding their dignity and wellbeing. In March 2016, paramilitary forces assassinated Cáceres in her home. Over the next several months, other activists, including Nelson Garcia and Lesiba Yaneth, were also murdered. The international furor over these killings among others pushed several financial sponsors of the proposed dam to withdraw their support. These activists and the community that surrounded them gave their lives for the sake of the wellbeing of the land they call home.

I do not mean to romanticize their deaths. Modern-day crucifixions are just as horrific as those two thousand years ago. It would have been better for such things not to have happened. Yet resistance was necessary when companies sought to maximize their profits at the Lenca's expense. These assassinations may have succeeded in their goal were it were not for the broader Lenca community's response. They didn't die for nothing; others were ready to press on for the cause. Individuals can be crushed. It's harder to kill movements. As Shane Claiborne of the New Monasticism movement and many others have said before, no one gets crucified for doing charity. It is only when one begins to question the systems of power, and even more than question them—to act and organize groups to resist such

---

evil systems—that crucifixion happens. How we communicate with others plays a great role in how broad such movements can become.

Being Right vs. Speaking to Your Audience

Educators know that people learn best when they can relate to or are hooked by the new information being presented to them. This is the power of analogy. Almost any new social insight I've ever learned started off as an analogy. For example, I distinctly remember visiting southern California for the first time and mentally comparing it to Israel/Palestine, which I'd visited while at seminary. That experience had left me feeling moved to work in solidarity with Palestinian Christians for their liberation from occupation. Months later, I was offered a church position in the San Diego area. I was struck at first by the topographical similarities, both being relatively dry, Mediterranean climates. I noticed the nice houses on hills with their tiled roofs, similar to Israeli settlements—and then I saw several encampments of migrant workers living at the bottom of the hills. My mind made the analogy: undocumented workers are the Palestinians of San Diego. Now, I recognize that this analogy is somewhat offensive. Undocumented workers should be understood on their own terms and not merely because one makes an analogy to another group one cares about. That's all true. But in that moment, I felt that the oppression the U.S. government was enabling in Palestine could also be fought in San Diego. My love for Palestinian Christians could perhaps be lived out best by fighting for justice closer to home, alongside immigrants in greater San Diego.

My understanding didn't stop there, but that's where it began. And frankly, I don't see any other way in which most people connect with issues. Sometimes I see activists filled with valid righteous indignation tell off a group of people who have said or done something ignorant, or remain generally oblivious to an injustice. From the perspective of the speaker, they are speaking truth to power, revealing uncomfortable realities, and criticizing their neighbors who should know better. To be committed to the wellbeing of an oppressed community in many ways demands a stance of tough love to those who are enabling injustice and violence.

However, often they are just "preaching to the choir." I see this dynamic a lot with online articles by activists. Those who already understand what's happening praise the author for their bravery and truth telling. The author probably feels that they are making a difference and fighting for their values. And if the goal is to be a witness for what they believe in, they have succeeded. If it is to mobilize the already converted, they may have succeeded, depending on follow through. But if the goal is to draw more people into the movement, they typically fail.

You have to speak to people where they are. You have to hook them by appealing to their experiences. If your goal is not education or building up new supporters, but is firing up the faithful, then you can declare "mission accomplished." The question is one of: Who is your audience? If your audience has nothing to associate with what you are saying, then you're unlikely to move them to action. Of course, there are exceptions to this rule. There have been times when someone has told me off very assertively. It affected me. It bothered me. If it really struck a nerve, it might stick with me for hours or a day. And I had two choices: (1) to dismiss that person as being a jerk, or (2) to delve more deeply into what they were saying. When the latter happened, it was because I had already built up a relationship with the speaker. I trusted their insights or concerns in some way. Seeing them so hot on a topic compelled me to learn more and not simply dismiss them. Now that I have more experience in justice activism, it's easier to be less defensive when reading a harshly worded article. I may not know the author, but if I care about the issue they are talking about, I take them seriously.

Now you should not have to police your tone when you write. But it is important that you recognize what you are doing. If you are interested in pedagogical efficacy, you need to speak to people where they are. You need to hook them. This is slow and often thankless work that can seem to take ages to bear fruit. And the urgency of issues often makes us feel that we don't have the time or energy for such slow, three-steps-forward, two-steps-back awareness raising and character formation. I wish it

> *You should not have to police your tone.*

were different, but that's the pattern I see over and over again. So long as people are clear on what they are trying to do, I don't see a problem with some of us handholding those whom we want to move and others of us throwing down the gauntlet. We have different roles and different gifts. We speak to and for different communities. What can feel like a blazing-hot challenge in one setting can be a run-of-the-mill talking point in another. At one church I've served, talking about confronting racism and working for racial justice is a standard Sunday occurrence. Somewhere else, it would be edgy or even controversial. Everyone is in different places, and I don't begrudge them for their social location. That doesn't mean we leave people where they are. It *does* mean speaking to where they are *now*, so that they may grow more faithful to the calling of the God of justice and compassion.

Quite often, we can be very self-centered in our own tragedies. This isn't surprising: we feel hardest what hits closest to us. But we don't have to be. Something may impact us quite personally, but not touch the next person. Likewise, if we are new to an issue and experiencing our first run-in with a problem, it's all the more important that we learn from others who've endured similar situations. Struggles don't start when *we* first "discover" them. Having a historical perspective is crucial. We do this, not in order to dismiss our own concerns, but to gain strength from witnessing and learning from generations past and ongoing struggles today. They are a great cloud of witnesses. Often oppressed and losing in the eyes of the world, they managed to survive and press on despite seeing no end to the evil they were facing. They endured through the strength they found in each other.

CHAPTER 4 DISCUSSION QUESTIONS

- How and where do you persevere?

- Besides the examples in this chapter, what are some other examples of communities who have persevered in the face of adversity? What is the good news that they proclaim?

- Have you ever tried verbally to make sense of another's suffering after hearing their story? Did the person respond positively to what you said, or did they resist your characterization?

- How can white Americans respond faithfully to the sin of racism? When is it best to speak, and when is it essential to remain silent and listen?

- What can we learn from those who have persevered in the face of oppression?

For Further Reading

Barber, William J. II, and Jonathan Wilson-Hartgrove. *The Third Reconstruction: How a Moral Movement Is Overcoming the Politics of Division and Fear*. Boston: Beacon Press, 2016.

Engler, Mark, and Paul Engler. *This Is an Uprising: How Nonviolent Revolt Is Shaping the Twenty-First Century*. New York: Nation Books, 2016.

Freire, Paulo. *Pedagogy of the Oppressed*. Translated by Donaldo Macedo. 30th Anniversary Edition. New York: Bloomsbury, 2000.

Jha, Sandhya Rani. *Pre-Post-Racial America: Spiritual Stories from the Front Lines*. St. Louis: Chalice Press, 2015.

Rieger, Joerg, and Kwok Pui-lan. *Occupy Religion: Theology of the Multitude*. Lanham, Md.: Rowman & Littlefield, 2012.

Slessarev-Jamir, Helene. *Prophetic Activism: Progressive Religious Justice Movements in Contemporary America*. New York: New York University Press, 2011.

Zinn, Howard. *A People's History of the United States*. New York: Harper Collins, 2003.

5

Communities Help Us Keep the Dream Alive

Toward the finale of the 2010 Pixar film *Toy Story 3*, the toys are in dire shape. Having made a daring escape from a day care center, they find themselves in a landfill. Caught on a conveyer belt, they are moving toward a giant incinerator. They try to scramble up the sides of loose, shredded garbage. Slowly but surely, they drift toward the incinerator. There is no escape. There is no way out. What will they do in this dire situation? One by one, they begin reaching out for each other and taking each other's hands until they all connect. Some call it one of the saddest moments in Pixar films, but it is also one of the most beautiful. When all seems lost, sometimes the best we can do is connect with each other. And that just might be enough.

Yet we typically want solutions that match the scale of our problems. Small problems need small solutions. Big problems need big solutions. Whether a problem is practical, social,

> *What if it's the case that big problems have inadequate and small solutions?*

or religious, this basic dynamic holds. For example, if the world is corrupt, people are evil, sin is pervasive, and humans are incapable of responding to God on their own, then we want a "big" solution—such as: Jesus Christ having sin crucified with him, triumphing over the powers of this world, and justifying us with grace in spite of ourselves. If you see our society as having small problems, it is reasonable to think that they can be addressed with small solutions. If the solution doesn't disrupt too many people's lives, then it is reasonable to think that it can be accomplished. For instance, maybe you see racism as a matter of private prejudice that comes out of people not knowing or listening to each other. If that is the case, then the solution is for people to listen to each other, thus helping racism diminish. We might call it the *Crash* solution, from the 2005 Oscar-winning film. In that movie, the message is that people can learn to get along if they stop yelling and instead listen to each other. It doesn't make sense to me, but admittedly it is compelling for many people. It's still wrong, though!

Alternatively, if you see the problem as far deeper, then the answers will more often require us to go to the roots of the problem. If the problem of racism is structures of privilege that are invisible to their beneficiaries and those who have a vested interest in not seeing how they unjustly benefit, the solution to *that* problem will be a far more than simple listening. Listening is how others hear the problem, not find the solution. If the problem of ecological sustainability is not simply recycling soft drink cans but transforming our economy and civilization away from the perpetual and accelerating accumulation of wealth, then the possibility of that being realized anytime soon is weakened. The crux of the matter is that, the more radical your answers become, the greater the likelihood that their full implementation becomes deferred, for years, decades, or generations.

I have noticed this pattern in justice organizations. The radical ones see the need for a deep-rooted transformation of our society—whether for immigrants, the incarcerated, the poor, or the planet. They can name the problems, analyze them, and make persuasive moral arguments about why things *ought* to be different. They might even be able to suggest rational policy changes that would provide a net benefit for communities at a reasonable cost. Yet we do not live in a world where a good argument automatically wins the day. The fact that something "ought" to be done and having the right ideas are rarely enough to get you over the finish line.

While trying to match problems and solutions makes sense on paper, I am suggesting a different approach. Call it the *Toy Story 3* approach, if you will. The problem is that the toys need to be rescued from destruction. Their solution is to reach out to each other. What if other big problems also have solutions that start with small, seemingly insufficient, steps? What if, as in the gospels, crucifixion is followed by a resurrection that is seen by only a few, and the Empire is still standing after the fact? Isn't that a description of our predicament?

Our world has incredible needs. We are facing overwhelming challenges. If, after we've given everything we've got, it's still not enough to fully resolve injustices, what do we do? What do we do when what we need is 100,000 people in the streets, but all we get is the same hundred already committed people? Of course, it's not always essential to have a huge number of people to make a measurable impact on society. Nevertheless, sometimes the best we can do is keep the dream alive that another world is possible.

While some people despair, and others abandon concrete transformational efforts for theoretical ideals, some radical activists do the work of maintaining a community that will support one another around their shared values. Such communities keep the dream alive that things don't have to be the way they are, that they can, in fact, be better. *The big idea of this book is that keeping alive the dream that things can be better is enough to sustain hope in an unjust world.* It isn't enough to keep us satisfied or cause us to become passive, because the struggle for justice and liberation continues. But it provides enough for us to endure, and it's meaningful enough to keep us going in the meantime on the way to a more just world.

We all struggle to press on sometimes. I admit I certainly do. Sometimes, activism goes dormant for periods before we get fired up again. I don't think it's feasible for most of us to be perpetually in activist mode. We may be dissatisfied with how things are, but it takes some spark to reignite our activism in its various forms. Over the long haul, it is crucial to be part of a community that holds common values and a common vision of how our world can be a healthier, more equitable place. Such groups are like the coals that keep the justice embers warm and ready to reignite a fire with the right fuel. Often, we need to keep such coals hot in fallow times (excuse the mixed metaphor!). For there are many false starts. Perhaps there is no greater false start than the perennial question among leftists of: "When will we replace capitalism with something better?"

When Overthrowing Capitalism Is Just Around the Corner

System change, not climate change! We are the 99 percent! People over profit! One cannot serve both God and wealth (Mt. 6:24)! Many slogans point to a growing awareness of the limits of America's economic system. Since the "Occupy" movement burst onto the scene in 2011, income and wealth inequality have become topics of renewed interest in the larger American public. Though it ultimately failed to achieve its grandest goals, Occupy was successful in helping create space for that debate to be reinvigorated.

The 2016 Democratic primary's debate about systems of inequality pushed this even further, threatening the presumptive frontrunner, Hillary Clinton, with what at first looked like a quixotic effort by the rumpled Senator Bernie Sanders. A candidate who originally looked like a sideshow became a serious threat. Did Sanders skip the media-training day, where you smile and speak in 30-second increments? He seemed to break the rules, talking about political and economic systems that had largely been considered sacrosanct. But there he was, generating youthful crowds on the need for a political revolution to fix a corrupt system with his stark Brooklyn accent. At a minimum, his campaign demonstrated that Americans are willing to question the institutions that maintain power and threaten the future of our planet for the sake of profit.

Capitalism is *resilient*. After so much energy spent and hours volunteered—after a Great Recession that rocked millions of people's misplaced confidence in the American system —we are where we are. Taxes are cut for powerful corporations and our safety net is further weakened. How will we respond? With whom will we connect? We need to do much more than make the occasional snarky tweet. It's time more of us get organized and start modeling how we want to see our world change.

Be the Change

In the 1986 film *The Mission*, 17th-century Catholic missionaries enter the Amazon. Through the language of music, they develop relationships with an indigenous community that converts to Christianity. One of the main characters, played by Robert DeNiro, is a former soldier who has a powerful conversion experience and joins the mission. Eventually, the Catholic Church leadership orders the missionaries to abandon their homes as the land is now desired by powerful political forces. Having internalized the missionaries' theology that the wilderness is evil, the indigenous people refuse to leave the village they have since built in the jungle. The missionaries have a choice: leave, or defy orders and stay. They choose to stay. But they have a second choice: to fight or to resist nonviolently the imminent arrival of military forces intent on destroying the village.

When you know you are going to lose, what should you do? How we respond in situations of weakness reveals who we are more than in moments of triumph. This is the issue facing both groups—the missionaries and the villagers—in the finale of *The Mission*. Some arm themselves and launch a sneak attack on the encroaching soldiers. Others remain at the church and village, praying and singing; when the soldiers finally arrive, they march unafraid in a processional with a crucifix held high above them. All of them—resisters violent and nonviolent alike—are violently killed. They lose. The question in effect is less, "What are we willing to do in order to win?" and more, "What are we to do in the face of losing?"

Our actions reveal our character, witness to how we see the world, and point to what we value in it. As someone who tries to follow the way of Jesus, this is what draws me to the gospel. While I frame it religiously, this instinct can also be expressed as part of a broader pattern called "prefigurative politics." Admittedly, it is a technical term. In essence, it simply means that we seek to embody the society in which we want to live, even if it is not historically realizable in the moment.

Some activists acknowledge that the *need* for revolutionary change is different than their immediate capacity to *realize* said revolution, whether they have in mind a spiritual, cultural, or political revolution (or all three!). When that is the case, prefigurative politics and prefigurative communities come to the fore. They envision, or attempt to live out, the values they want the larger society to express. Think of intentional communities in the vein of Shane Claiborne's New Monastic Movement—groups such as Catholic Worker communities, left-wing Mennonites, Jewish *kibbutzim,* or Gandhi-inspired *ashrams.* We can likewise include secular groups that hold a common vision and support each other in that struggle for meaning and endurance "in the meantime," even if that meantime is a perpetual extension of an unfulfilled need of liberation. Such communes or communities offer a space to embody on a small scale the type of relationships people hope will eventually structure their world.

Our dominant society does not make it easy to form healthy community. Most of us in the United States do not belong to such tightly woven groups; we are increasingly fragmented. Many books have been written about the loss of civic culture in which groups interact on a face-to-face basis. Whether it is the decline of amateur sports teams or local community organizing changes in neighborhoods, we feel more dispersed. While the Internet and social media culture have allowed us to connect with people with niche interests around the world, it can't replace face-to-face interactions over years and decades. This is particularly true when grievances have a significant spatial dimension. Geographic dispersal can work against us when injustice is concentrated in a particular area.

In some ways, it may be easier to form community in smaller towns where most everyone knows each other, or in tight-knit neighborhoods in metro areas where cultural norms other than the dominant society continue to play major roles, but by and large we are increasingly distant from one another. Social media is both a blessing and curse in this dynamic: it makes it easier for disparate individuals to connect around shared interests on an international level, but it also alienates us from our place and those immediately around us. How many of us have had someone nearly bump into us on the sidewalk with their nose buried in their smartphone? Or had to say something repeatedly to a loved one in the same room who is too busy to notice us because they are habitually checking Facebook updates? Maybe even we ourselves have been distracted during a meeting, retreat, or family meal by receiving constant texts and feeling a compulsive instinct to *respond now*.

For most of my adult life, I have been drawn to the need for intentional community. My favorite living situation was on a seminary campus. I had my own space—kitchen, bathroom, bedroom—but there were 40 other people just down the hall or a flight of stairs away. It was expected that we would gather for a meal at least once a week, chapel several times a week, and a fellowship/fun event once a week. So, when my wife and I moved to the Los Angeles area, we looked for prospective intentional communities and briefly considered moving to one. We visited one prospective intentional community. It was a nice group of people, but the wrong kind of intentional community for us at that stage of our lives. Most of its members were significantly younger than us, mostly right out of college, and all of them were single. The single biggest drawback was that the only private spaces members had were their bedrooms. We were open to a shared kitchen (my spouse had lived for a year at a collective housing site while in grad school, which had a shared kitchen), but the shared bathroom was too much for us.

There are many styles of intentional community, with different rules of order or disciplines. Some try to share everything—such as "The Farm" in Tennessee that came out of the hippie movement and evolved over time away from total collectivism. Others have separate houses but live on a single street or neighborhood block. I dream of a time when we can be part of an intentional community that includes a variety of life stages and stations in life. Whatever form such communities take, each one is an example of a prefigurative community. They live out as best they can the vision of how they want to see our world change. Beyond the solely practical, such models require symbols and images that inspire their actions. There is great power in religious symbols in strengthening community, including those found in the Bible, but we must not use them uncritically.

On Using Biblical Imagery and Rhetoric

Communities need symbols to motivate their organization and activities. Symbols help form meaning, but can come at the high cost of regulating who's *inside* and who's *outside*. This is especially risky when using biblical imagery and rhetoric. "Prooftexting" is an example of this: when someone takes a verse from the Bible out of context to argue the validity of a predetermined point of view. Rarely do people acknowledge they are doing this. They just launch into a declaration that, "The Bible says…" End of discussion. This is particularly frustrating when you are trying to make a point about what the gospel demands more broadly. Themes of justice, equality, and compassion sometimes occur in a single verse, but more often than not they appear as broader themes and images that can't be easily boiled down to a single quoted line. For example, we might say the Bible teaches us how God loves and welcomes everyone and invites us to do likewise. Diverse sexual orientations and gender identities are therefore a blessing from God, and God has a special concern for those who experience oppression and marginalization in their society. But a more conservative Christian will likely quote verses such as Romans 1:26–27 or Leviticus 18:22 back at us. When taken literally, such verses point away from the broader, more inclusive priorities of the gospel. They are discussion-closers rather than discussion-starters.

The debate is often about which biblical verses to cite. For example, discussions about the need to reduce poverty in our communities have strong backing throughout the Bible, with several thousand individual verses highlighting how poverty hurts people and is against God's will. God desires righteousness among God's people, which means living ethically as a community. Not allowing poverty in the midst of plenty is an obvious application of that theme. Nevertheless, someone is always bound to retort: "The poor you will always have with you," quoting Jesus in Matthew 26:11 (NIV). Paraphrasing Jim Wallis, the founder of the progressive evangelical group Sojourners: The poor will always be with us only because of our hardened hearts, not because God desires that some people remain poor!

We are stuck at an impasse. Even clear injunctions from Jesus, such as "loving your enemies," have their own rejoinders elsewhere in the

Bible to "drive evildoers from your midst." Some thoughtful people, such as Dan Schultz, a United Church of Christ pastor who writes regularly for *Religious Dispatches* online magazine, has concluded that this whole process is not worth the effort. Few people are emotionally swayed by citing this or that passage. The effect is more akin to rooting for your team. As Schultz says:

> The number of scripture verses you can quote doesn't matter a bit. Nor does how many more of those verses speak of social justice than sexual ethics. It does not matter how "prophetic" people are. Nor does it matter how spirituality informs one's politics. We live in a secular and hyper-partisan age. These things motivate almost no one.[1]

Ouch. For me, the pertinent question is: Do we deploy religious language and imagery, or give up those symbols to conservative Christians? It seems that the issue Schultz is most animated about is a certain passivity or naïveté among progressive Christians that, if we could only come together and use reason, we could heal our nation and make everything all right. Fair enough. Reasoning is not the means by which change happens; doing—organizing and resisting oppression—matters more.

So, how do we use the Bible to frame issues, and to what effect? Using biblical passages and imagery can indeed be persuasive to people who are on the fence. I've seen this shift occur with public officials or business executives who witnessed a foot-washing ceremony for workers that emphasized the latter's dignity and value. On at least one occasion, an official heard me quoting 20th-century Christian ethicist Reinhold Niebuhr during public testimony and came up to me afterward and mentioned how they appreciated what I had to say. The imagery helped strengthen their resolve to support our demands on behalf of victims of police misconduct.

Expressing larger biblical themes can also have a powerful effect—themes such as that of an exodus out of oppressive situations,

---

[1] Dan Schultz. "Maybe Instead of Solidarity, the Religious Left Should Try Being Indivisible," *Religion Dispatches,* posted June 20, 2017, http://religiondispatches. org/maybe-instead-ofsolidarity- the-religious-left-should-try-being-indivisible/.

traveling in the wilderness, journeying to the promised land, facing crucifixion, the hope for resurrection in our society, and the kingdom of God. Such "religious scaffolding" provides a framework from which to interpret various issues. Obviously, the ones I mention are specific to the Christian tradition, but there are many other ways of morally persuading people through other images, such as Buddhist "Enlightenment" or fulfilling the role of a "Bodhisattva." Such imagery can help to motivate someone who is passively supportive, but hesitant to act. It can also help to shape hearts in a one-to-one setting.

But such imagery's most important effect is in witnessing to one's values and understanding of what the gospel demands. They can, for example, frame the priorities of a faith community. The faith organizer Alexia Salvatierra, a leader in the Matthew 25 immigration movement, has again and again cited Jesus' admonition to "be wise as serpents and innocent as doves" (Mt. 10:16). I understand this to mean two things: First, we need to do a careful calculation and analysis in determining the obstacles to the things we want to see accomplished in our society. This involves incentives and speaking to people's perceived self-interest. Most classic community organizing follows this approach. Second, we need to trust that hearts can be turned through the power of the Spirit, *beyond* our calculations and pressure. This means invoking religious symbols and language, doing rituals that move hearts, and praying for our opponents and those we wish to change. We have to be hardnosed in speaking about people's interests, but we should not fool ourselves that narrow self-interest is the only thing that motivates people.

Moral persuasion doesn't take seriously enough the degree to which evil is intransigent to any change that seeks to restrict its power. If we think that quoting Jesus and offering a prayer is the end of wisdom, we are sorely mistaken. It is only the *beginning* of wisdom. We know who we are and whose we are. From there, we proceed to the ongoing journey of participating in God's struggle for a more just earth through hard thinking and persistence. And then we can look back at this work and interpret it through other biblical imagery that helps motivate us to persist. In strengthening community for the long haul, we reclaim the imagery that inspires us.

Keep on Keeping On

A key insight in the struggle for social justice and transformation is expressed in the traditional African American spiritual "There Is a Balm in Gilead." It says:

> *Sometimes I feel discouraged*
> *and think my work's in vain*
> *but then the Holy Spirit*
> *revives my soul again.*

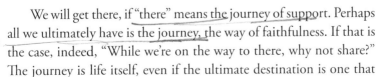

This is exactly right. We will feel down. We will feel despair. These feelings are not signs of unfaithfulness. They reflect realistic responses to a world that is wounded, that is filled with the sins of oppression and injustice. Even so:

> *There is a balm in Gilead*
> *to make the wounded whole;*
> *there is a balm in Gilead*
> *to heal the sin-sick soul.*

God desires for us to be healed from what wounds us, to wound others less, and to uplift our souls pressed down by evil. I have suggested throughout this book that communities are one essential way in which hope can endure. Of course, God sometimes meets us personally when we are feeling alone. But more often than not, the Spirit is present when at least two or three are gathered together.

While secular in origin, another song in which I find this insight is "He Ain't Heavy, He's My Brother," by the Hollies. The singer reflects on our ability to help one another in the struggle of life, implying that through our mutual support we strengthen one another. The journey of life continues. The welfare of our "brother" is worth our concern:

> *No burden is he to bear*
> *We'll get there*

We will get there, if "there" means the journey of support. Perhaps all we ultimately have is the journey, the way of faithfulness. If that is the case, indeed, "While we're on the way to there, why not share?" The journey is life itself, even if the ultimate destination is one that is always just beyond the horizon. The journey is not as much of a burden when we travel it with others.

Newbie Activism

The term "newbie" has somewhat pejorative connotations. Most frequently expressed in video or board game culture, it means someone who is just being introduced to the game. While others have devoted much of their waking energy at devising strategies to be better, more effective players, some are coming in cold. They don't know the rules. They don't know what has worked well for others. They are experimenting. They make mistakes. But there is nothing wrong with beginning something or being a newcomer. Like any activity, having new blood in your group is vital for new ideas to bubble up and prevent things from becoming stale. You may even consider yourself an activist newbie. Maybe you attended your first rally just this past year. You were living your life, doing your thing, and something clicked. You found that you were driven, pushed, led internally to go out and do something. It could have been a rally, a candlelight vigil, a march with a homemade sign, or a gathering on a street corner. You might have traveled across the state, to the other side of the country, or just a few blocks from where you live. Regardless of the specifics, you went out there and did something.

Often, that first action is critical to whether you continue your engagement. If you had an uplifting experience, you probably felt empowered and excited for the next opportunity to make your voice known. If you felt belittled or dismissed, or if the energy or attendance at the event was especially low, you may have thought, "Screw that. I have better things to do with my time." In the summer of 2017, I carpooled with two strangers to an interfaith rally against white supremacy. One person in the carpool was organizing a big event in a few months, and the other person was attending their first action ever. I asked the second person why she was attending the event. She said she had always tried to be a kind person, care for others, and show her values through her personal actions. But increasingly it wasn't feeling like it was enough. She wanted to do more. With white supremacists openly marching around the country, and her being a woman who had emigrated from Mexico, she felt like she needed to attend this rally. She appeared nervous but excited about putting herself out there for justice.

We separated for the duration of the rally. Once it concluded and it was time to carpool back together, I didn't see her. The other activist who drove us said she had found another ride, so I messaged her afterward to hear her reaction. She was motivated. She was on fire. She was so moved and ready to go to another action. She was going to invite her friends and family to the next action. Her excitement rejuvenated me. It was the passion of a newbie activist, for whom the possibilities seem endless. Our country needs to see more such awakenings.

Sometimes, veterans of social justice campaigns or direct actions are condescending to newbie activists. Some have been active for decades, from the civil rights movement to women's rights and Vietnam, to the environmental movement and gay rights, to anti-nuclear activism and supporting Central American refugees, on to gun control, accessibility work, and so forth. Or maybe they have been deeply rooted in a single struggle for a decade or more. Once in a while, I read articles from veteran activists about new people coming into a movement. A few of them say something along the lines of, "Where were they when such-and-such was going on? That can drive people away. Instead, we should be trying to figure out: "How do we keep people hooked?"

> *We need to do a better job of welcoming newcomers into the cause.*

Newcomers are looking for meaning and belonging in order to stay engaged. Walking people through the history of an issue can more deeply ground them in what's been going, and in the wisdom of ancestors and those who have gone before us. This practice helps avoid being ahistorical; your personal "aha" moment is not the only lens through which to see an issue. But to lambast a potential partner for their perceived lateness to the cause is counter-productive. Not unlike Jesus's observation that he who is without sin should cast the first stone, each of us should be reminded that we are all latecomers to someone else's struggle. Maybe we lived someplace else, maybe we were complicit in another's oppression, maybe we simply hadn't been *born* yet. There is always someone who preceded us. For those who are new, this perspective invites us to a certain humility and openness to learn from the wisdom of activist elders. For veterans, it's a reminder to try to remember what it was like when everything felt brand new and it seemed that the scales had fallen off your eyes for the first time (Acts 9:18).

I can recall times when I had such "aha" moments. But I also remember how my thoughts on them have evolved over time. I expect that dealing with me was frustrating in the early days for those whose justice struggle was longstanding. For example, I never gave much thought to the concerns of undocumented immigrants or their families until the summer of 2005, when I was well into my 20s. Even though I had taken undergraduate courses in the areas of Spanish and Government on topics concerning Latin America, I didn't know much about recent immigrants to the United States. I could tell you about the U.S.'s unjust interventions through the 19th and 20th centuries: coups in Guatemala, migration from the impact of NAFTA, United Fruit Company's political and economic dominance in Latin America, and I could give a great critique of the Pinochet regime of Chile that had U.S. backing. Even so, this was academic knowledge and I didn't know anything about immigration to the U.S. per se. I had met immigrants, looking back, but I didn't have the framework to understand them as such. There was David's mom from Venezuela, Nabeel's family from Saudi Arabia, and Biton's parents from India by way of Chicago, but the category of "immigrants" was largely invisible to my eyes.

Only when placed in a context of agricultural work on the Yakama Indian Reservation where recent immigrants from Mexico did most of the farm labor was I confronted with how much I didn't understand. I had lived in places that were mainly black and white. So, being exposed to the experience of Mexican immigrants, many of whom were either undocumented or had a parent who was undocumented, was a revelation. I had no framework by which to engage in any sort of activism regarding immigrant rights because it was a category of which I was not even aware. Soon thereafter, immigrant rights would make national headlines with the Sensenbrenner Bill, a draconian piece of work that led to the mobilization of millions of immigrants who had previously been largely invisible to the broader American public.

We rarely know when we will receive our wakeup call. For many immigration activists, the massive response to the Sensenbrenner Bill was the genesis moment that still reverberates today. But even *then*, I wasn't really engaged in immigrant rights while living in St. Louis. I remember hearing about the May action my second year in seminary, but the downtown St. Louis rally only had a few hundred people in attendance. Few if any progressive seminarians went to it, even among those committed to social justice. It wasn't until I moved to California and started serving in a church in an area with many immigrants that supporting immigrants became more than a stance of passive intellectual support. But for those who were involved in immigrant and refugee rights during the first Sanctuary Movement in the 1980s, activists coming into their own in 2005 and 2006 were Johnny-come-latelies.

It sometimes makes veteran activists feel good to say how we were involved before something was well known. It gives us a certain sense of authenticity. Call it a hipster activist sensibility. *Oh, you are speaking out against the U.S.'s bombings in Syria? I've been arguing against the U.S. being militarily involved in the Middle East since 2002, a year before the second invasion of Iraq.* Such condescending attitudes don't help expand the supporters to a cause. In fact, they tend to drive people away. If we seek to demonstrate the purity of our cause, or to be an exclusive group, then this stance is justified. But if we want to educate people and help them become better activists, we have to meet them where they are. Later on, historical context and trainings on how issues have endured over time are surely critical. But if we expect people to know the full background before they take the first step, the majority will likely leave before they begin. That may make us feel good—believing that they weren't truly here for the right reasons to begin with, which may be true. Yet can we really maintain the stance that someone's motivations must be utterly pure before they become involved? If we are honest with ourselves, were our own motivations pure when we began? Are they even now? Meeting people where they are at, and inviting them to journey more deeply into causes of justice, is part of their own development. It is a good thing if it means the movement is more influential. We need to do a better job of welcoming newcomers into the cause.

At the same time, we should beware of contributing to newcomer burnout by demanding too much of fellow activists, especially newbies. Someone comes to an action or cause, fired up and ready to change the world. That kind of energy is helpful in coming up with new ideas and bringing new bodies to events. At the same time, it must be tempered—not as in "diminished," but like steel being purified through fire. Institutional will endures longer than a lone individual's passions can burn bright. Systems are slow to change. In fact, they tend to hold on until they go through a sudden shift or collapse.

Compare social change movement to that of a seesaw. We all know how one works. If you place a hundred-pound weight on the left side of a seesaw with no countervailing weight, that side will drop to the ground while the right side will rise up. Think of a system of inequity and injustice as that hundred-pound weight. Activism and the power it generates are the weight added to the right side of the seesaw. Without them, it remains up in the air. Maybe after a year of activism through phone calls, organizing neighbors, sending delegations to officials, and having marches, we manage to add 20 pounds to the right side. But the seesaw will still look the same. It won't move. Add another 20 pounds, and then another, and then another, and still you only have 80 pounds of organizing pressure. The seesaw still won't move. At that point, many people may say to themselves, "Things are hopeless! We'll never get things to change." If only they knew how close they were! Once the right side of the seesaw has just a little over hundred pounds as a counterweight, you will see big movements in a short amount of time. But it requires sticking with it through the tough times, when it feels as if you are losing; it means we keep going when we want to give up; and it means being able to evaluate realistically where things stand.

That kind of endurance is hard to foster. We want quick fixes, and the kind of multiyear commitment this type of change requires is hard to come by. In the meantime, we have to wrestle with feelings of despair and hopelessness. Even in the fights that ultimately triumph, there are still often setbacks. From a certain perspective, someone trying to tip that seesaw is going to appear to be losing right up to the pivot point, the moment when things change. To evaluate progress, we need criteria that are less obvious than a moving seesaw. There will be setbacks. We are going to lose—a lot. And there are no guarantees that the time, effort, and sacrifices we spend will result in the changes we so desire. Communities help us keep the dream alive in the meantime. They are valuable in and of themselves for that reason alone. Just as there are a seemingly infinite number of issues we can attach ourselves to, there are innumerable existing organizations to choose from. So, when should we join an already existing group, and when should we start something new? Read on.

Starting vs. Joining

Americans like to think of themselves as innovators, as people who don't want to do something the same way just because it has always been done that way. That instinct has led to many creative changes, new jobs, and movements over the years. But it has also separated us from positive things that have come before or are ongoing. We are increasingly hesitant to join something that someone else started. We want to do our own thing, start afresh. When it comes to forming community, should we join one that already exists, and maybe has for multiple generations, or should we create something new? This dilemma holds regardless of whether we are talking about joining a justice organization or a religious congregation. (A quiz on whether to start or join follows this section.)

Whether you find an already existing group or have to start a new one, it matters that the members of the group agree with the reason or vision of why it exists. People can be in agreement about the need to respond to some issue but still have radically different perspectives on how it should be addressed. Some may want to form an all-online advocacy network. Others may want to initiate a grassroots door-knocking program in neighborhoods as a means to building community. Some may feel the need to focus on internal support of group members, while others will want to emphasize reaching out to those not yet connected and engaged. Compromise is important, and we can all benefit from listening better to others' perspectives. We gain much from one another. If each demand total unanimity, we will quickly have organizations of a single member each. The result would be not unlike the movie *The Life of Brian,* in which the different radical Jewish liberation groups all hate the occupying Romans, but can't get along with each other. The Judean People's Front, the People's Front of Judea, and the Popular Front all hate each other, calling each other "splitters." We can take new group creation and fragmentation to the extreme: I once heard that there were approximately 36 distinct Marxist parties in Argentina. Purity of purpose can go too far.

In spite of the risk of fragmentation, there comes a time when people have to go their separate ways. Especially if the group is activist-oriented, we have to limit what is our focus and what is not. This happens with faith communities and congregations too. Part of their purpose is to show how even radically different persons and groups can still come together in fellowship and love. Part of their power as symbols is when they successfully bring together a cross-section of people who are inspired to work together and support one another in a common effort. Done well, they can inspire many and reflect in microcosm a better society. They prefigure the world as we want it to be.

Whether activist, religious, or both, it is still hard to know whether to join a group that already exists or start again anew. Below is a little quiz to help you decide what is the best approach for you.

"Starting a New Group" Questionnaire

INSTRUCTIONS: Answer each yes/no question, proceeding along the path of questions until you reach an end result.

1. Are you currently participating in some organization or community?
   [*If yes, proceed to question #2. If no skip to question #4.*]

2. Is this community helping you find meaning and/or accomplish what you feel led to do?
   [If yes, stop!]
   Recommendation: Stick with it and help make it the best group it can be!
   [If no, proceed to question #3.]

3. Do you have the energy and drive to help change this group into something life giving?
   [If yes, stop!]
   Recommendation: Stick with it and help make it the best group it can be!
   [If no, proceed to question #4.]

4. Have you looked around to see if there is a group that reflects your commitments?
   [If no, stop!]
   Recommendation: Do your homework.
   [If yes, proceed to question #5.]

5. Did you find some that fit?
   [If yes, stop!]
   Recommendation: Give them a try. In a few months, return to question #2.
   [If no, proceed to question #6.]

6. Are you willing to organize and invite people around an interest that you see is not being met?
   [If yes, stop!]
   Recommendation: Start a new group or community!
   [If no, proceed to question #7.]

7. If there is no group around and you don't have the energy to start something, you have three options:
   A. Wait and see.
   B. Find another need or interest.
   C. Give up.
   Recommendation: Take the quiz again in six months.

What Affects One Directly Affects All Indirectly

My favorite religious letter is not one that appears in the Bible (even though I value Paul's insights). Rather, it is the Rev. Dr. Martin Luther King Jr.'s "Letter from a Birmingham Jail." In addition to highlighting the hypocrisy of supposedly moderate religious leaders who critiqued the civil rights movement's nonviolent direct action tactics, he makes some broader claims that transcend that moment. He writes, "Whatever affects one directly, affects all indirectly. I can never be what I ought to be until you are what you ought to be. This is the interrelated structure of reality." Some say this is merely a beautiful metaphor about solidarity, perhaps something to hang on the wall in your kitchen. But I actually think it's true. Its claim makes a demand of us; it reveals something about the nature of existence to us. Solidarity with one another, especially those experiencing oppression, is part of our own wellbeing. We ignore it at our peril.

My own academic research has been rooted largely in understanding and being able to explain *how* King's words are true. For the vast majority of us, the assertion is more than enough. The main point is not even to convince others of the intellectual veracity of King's claim—it's for people to experience it and practice it. If we live this value, we experience its truth for ourselves.

We need each other. I need you. You need others, for, without them, you don't even know what you are missing in terms of your own growth and healing. Arguments can only get us so far, a bit like someone arguing with a skeptic about whether God exists. The best result one can expect is that the skeptic will have found the conversation to be intellectually stimulating. But there is a world of difference between talking about God as an intellectually credible option and experiencing that love from and with others in your life. The same goes for King's sense of solidarity. To know this truth is to know in your deepest sense of self that you are wrapped up in others' wellbeing and they in yours. To wound another is to wound yourself. To bind up the broken parts of another helps to bind up those broken parts of yourself too. This is the truest meaning of that most famous commandment, "You shall love your neighbor as yourself" (Mk. 12:31).

This recognition of our interwoven nature is another reason why we cannot do without communities. They constitute a large portion of who we are. Thriving communities lead to thriving persons. A hurting community ripples pain throughout its members and those shaped by it. To endure in a world where the value of others is so consistently dismissed or seen as expendable for the sake of more financially profitable values, we *need* each other. I know I would have given up a long time ago without the witness of so many other people who have shaped me. We give each other strength, showing that this world of both joy and pain is still worth fighting for, come what may. We have a long way to go, with no final destination. If the journey is everything, we had better learn to support each other along the way.

A Mountain with No Top

I am not a huge fan of Saul Alinsky, the founder of modern community organizing models. More accurately, I'm not a fan of his disciples, who laud his methods as the *single* right way to accomplish real change, something that Alinsky himself would have disdained. But I really find compelling his vision of the struggle in which we are engaged. There are no final victories, no once and forever achievements of social salvation. There are moments of triumph, which even within them hold the seeds to counter-reactions and new struggles. He describes this process of incompletion like a journey up a mountain, saying:

> If we think of the struggle as a climb up a mountain, then we must visualize a mountain with no top. We see a top, but when we finally reach it, the overcast rises and we find ourselves merely on a bluff. The mountain continues on up. Now we see the "real" top ahead of us, and strive for it, only to find we've reached another bluff, the top still above us. And so it goes on, interminably.[2]

---

[2]Saul Alinsky, *Rules for Radicals: A Pragmatic Primer for Realistic Radicals* (1971; New York: Vintage Books, 1989), 21.

You may find that frustrating, but it's the world we live in: the unavoidable condition of a justice-seeking existence. We will reach new bluffs and achievements that future generations will look back on as "backwards." For some, marriage equality was the realization of the American Dream. Others may see the end to mass incarceration of people of color, resolving climate change, or ending extreme poverty as the "be all, end all." In religious terms, we call this "the Eschaton," in which the Divine is revealed fully here on earth. Each of these goals is a worthy mountaintop vision; each is but a bluff in a never-ending journey.

We are indeed the hands and feet of God, but we are not the only hands and feet. Our group, ministry, or community is one of countless hands—untold numbers—that are being perpetually invited to respond to the needs of our world for the sake of greater value, diversity, and affirmation. Call it the "body of Christ" if you will. When we say no or ignore the call, there are other hands ready to respond. Of course, that does not let us off the hook. We are responsible for what we do as the would-be hands of God, and we are responsible for what we leave undone. This includes helping right the wrongs of the past and assisting other faithful hands in building up the divine commonwealth.

Whatever the limitations we face in achieving a world that more fully reflects God's will on earth as it is in heaven, perhaps there is no greater limitation than the feeling of being alone, the feeling that there is nothing we can do—that it's hopeless, so why even try? Such fatalism can kill any efforts before they begin, perversely justifying the cynicism that enabled them. It is easy to feel hopeless and alone. Yet such

> *There are no final victories, no once and forever achievements of social salvation.*

feelings can be mitigated partially through a community that supports and loves you, and through you doing the same in return. It's not simply that we cheer each other up; it's that we cheer each other on.

Lament happens in community. We often grieve alone, but we lament collectively. To be able to name the pain we have felt, see that others acknowledge that pain and feel similarly—such responses can lessen the stings of an unjust world. More so, they can help us cling to the truth that it doesn't have to be this way—such hopeful dreams cannot be sustained alone.

The power of community, though, is not a cure-all. There will be inevitable struggles and failures, many that will shake our conviction that another world is possible. And yet, even in the worst-case scenario, if the whole world goes up in flames, we can still reach out to each other, letting one another know that we are not alone. We might be 11 people hiding from the authorities in an upper room. We might be saying goodbye as our community is dispersed through gentrification. We might be a dying church or community that's on its last call before the lights go out. We might be a set of toys edging our way toward the incinerator. But that doesn't mean that we are forgotten. That doesn't mean that God is done with us, or our world, yet.

Because, even when there is a crucifixion, there is another day, a resurrection of new possibilities. It may not be for us, or for those we know, but God is never done with us. God takes our world, looks at the mess we make of it, and each other, and says, "Well, what should we do next?" And so another moment becomes available. For, just as the dream is never fully realized, the dream can never die. Christ can never be killed once and for all. The divine commonwealth is always just around the next bend, just past the next mountaintop, inviting us to live like it's here now. Because, when we live like God's dreams have already won, then we can truly sustain hope in an unjust world.

CHAPTER 5 DISCUSSION QUESTIONS

- What was it like when you joined a new group, and what are ways to make "newbies" feel welcome in the groups or activities in which you are already engaged?

- How can communities better keep alive the dream that another world is possible?

- Where have you seen your community do this successfully? What did it feel like to be part of that community, even if you didn't "win"?

- How can your congregation or community better exemplify in its daily living this ideal of keeping the dream of a just world alive?

- How could keeping the dream alive be something that motivates others to be part of your community?

For Further Reading

Alinsky, Saul D. *Rules for Radicals: A Practical Primer for Realistic Radicals.* New York: Random House, 1971.

Claiborne, Shane. *The Irresistible Revolution: Living as an Ordinary Radical.* Grand Rapids, Mich.: Zondervan, 2006.

Cobb, John B. Jr., ed. *Resistance: The New Role of Progressive Christians.* Louisville: Westminster John Knox Press, 2008.

King, Martin Luther Jr. "Letter from Birmingham Jail." In *Why We Can't Wait,* 85–110. 1964. Reprint, Boston: Beacon Press, 2011.

Murphy, Timothy. *Counter-Imperial Churching for a Planetary Gospel: Radical Discipleship for Today.* Anoka, Minn.: Process Century Press, 2017.

Salvatierra, Alexia, and Peter Hetzel. *Faith-Rooted Organizing: Mobilizing the Church in Service to the World.* Downers Grove, Ill.: InterVarsity Press, 2014.

Wink, Walter. *Engaging the Powers: Discernment and Resistance in a World of Domination.* Minneapolis: Fortress Press, 1992.

THEOLOGICAL LEANINGS QUIZ RESULTS

A. Secular Humanist

B. Evangelical

C. Adherent of the Prosperity Gospel

D. Liberal Protestant

E. Liberation-Relational Disciple

When there's so much conflict around the country and around the corner, it's easy to feel overwhelmed and helpless.

What can one person do to make a difference?

"This is a book to be cherished." —Eboo Patel

TRANSFORMING COMMUNITIES

How People Like You Are Healing Their Neighborhoods

Sandhya Rani Jha

ISBN 9780827237155

Take heart and be inspired by real stories of ordinary people who took action and changed their corner of the world, one block at a time. Equal parts inspiration, education, and do-it-yourself, *Transforming Communities* will open your eyes to the world-healing potential within you, and give you the vision, the tools, and the encouragement to start transforming *your* neighborhood.

ChalicePress.com   800-366-3383

"Visionary, yet down-to-earth. Theologically perceptive, and highly practical. This is a book the church needs to read."

—Michael Kinnamon, former General Secretary, National Council of Churches

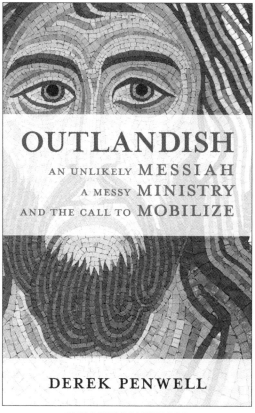

ISBN 9780827231665

Jesus did everything wrong. Ministering to the wrong people. Expecting outrageous commitment from his followers. Questionable teaching methods. A humiliating end followed by an improbable surprise ending. And then, somehow, inspiring millions to attempt to change the world in his name.

ChalicePress.com   800-366-3383

The 21st century is the age of community organizing, from rallies in the streets to online movements for change. What if congregations embraced community organizing?

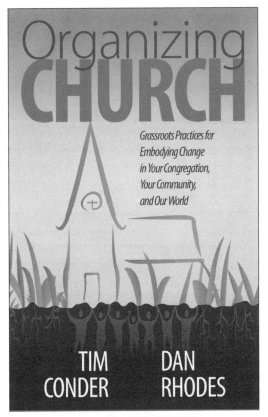

ISBN 9780827227637

Organizing Church offers a unique perspective that blends proven principles of community organizing and research on socially active congregations into a formula that will revitalize and empower churches as change-agents.

ChalicePress.com   800-366-3383

"Michael W. Waters... is both blunt and lyrical as he meditates on police violence, racism, hip-hop, and the power of faith."
—*Sojourners*

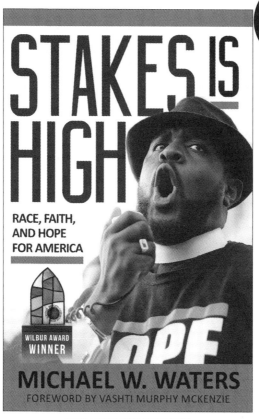

ISBN 9780827235403

Dallas pastor, community leader, and activist Michael Waters weaves stories of the past and present to create a sense of urgency for the need for racial justice in America today. Listen to the stories and join the work for justice.

Part of the Forum for Theological Exploration series.

ChalicePress.com   800-366-3383

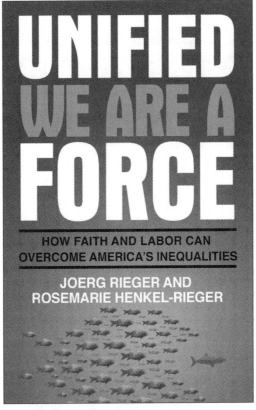

ISBN 9780827238589

The American dream of "pulling yourself up by your bootstraps" is no longer possible, if it ever was. Most of us live paycheck to paycheck, and inequality has become one of the greatest problems facing our country. Working people and people of faith have the power to change this—but only when we get unified!

ChalicePress.com   800-366-3383

30 new sermons to empower your prophetic voice for solidarity and justice

ISBN 9780827231597

As nationalism, patriarchy, and alt-right fearmongering threaten our troubled nation, the pulpit has again become a subversive space of sacred resistance. In this provocative and powerful collection of sermons from diverse pastors across America, hear the brave and urgent voice of Christians calling for radical change rooted in love, solidarity, and justice.

ChalicePress.com   800-366-3383

"Helsel gets what so many preachers—
and the congregations they serve—so
desperately need in these critical times."

—Brian McLaren, author and activist

"This book is spot-on for the kinds of conversations
we need to be having."
– Walter Brueggemann, author of Sabbath as Resistance

ANXIOUS
TO TALK
ABOUT IT

Helping White Christians
Talk Faithfully about Racism

CAROLYN B. HELSEL

PREACHING
ABOUT

RACISM

A GUIDE FOR
FAITH LEADERS

CAROLYN B. HELSEL

ISBN 9780827200722   ISBN 9780827231627

Drawing from more than a decade of work with
white congregations on race issues, professor and pastor
Carolyn B. Helsel explores and engages the anxiety many
Christians experience about racism and paves a way forward
for more informed, compassionate, and healing conversations.

ChalicePress.com   800-366-3383